Nina Edwards is a freelance writer and author of *Offal* (forthcoming, 2012). She is an actor and has taught at a Japanese University. She lives in London.

For Mary and Gordon Hedley Salmon

Onthebutton
The Significance of an Ordinary Item

NINA EDWARDS

LONDON · NEW YORK

Published in 2012 by I.B.Tauris & Co Ltd
6 Salem Road, London W2 4BU
175 Fifth Avenue, New York NY 10010
www.ibtauris.com

Distributed in the United States and Canada
Exclusively by Palgrave Macmillan
175 Fifth Avenue, New York NY 10010

ISBN: 978 1 84885 584 7

A full CIP record for this book is available from the British Library
A full CIP record is available from the Library of Congress

Library of Congress Catalog Card Number: available

Printed and bound in Great Britain by TJ International Ltd, Padstow,
Cornwall

CONTENTS

LIST OF ILLUSTRATIONS

19. Watercolour on ivory of a boy, possibly Sir Frederick Augustus d'Este, 1794–1848, by Richard Cosway. The buttoned skeleton suit demonstrates new attitudes towards children – or children of a certain privileged class – who should, for example, enjoy more freedom of movement in their dress. V&A (P.7-1941). • 8 9

20. Woman's Transformation Suit: double-breasted reefer jacket in grey wool boxcloth, 1892–1897. Masculine tailoring betrayed by fancy revers and applied Russian braid – but simple manlike shell coat buttons. V&A (T.70-1954). • 9 2

21. Ann Carrington, *Crown Jewels*, buttons on canvas, 205 × 140 cm, 2010. • 1 0 7

22. *All things Bright*, photographic print 92 × 117 cm, Kate Kessling, 2009. Pretty pastel colours: fancy mini cakes, iced biscuits, jelly cubes, a cute guinea pig and buttons. • 1 1 7

23. Dog's teeth with silver button backs, which are more likely fond mementos of a beloved companion, worn in somewhat macabre respect. Private collection. Photograph JMB. • 1 4 6

24. *Mourning Eye*, photographic print, 52 × 75 cm, Kate Kessling, 2009. • 1 5 3

25. Jet mourning buttons and a photograph of them being worn, late nineteenth century. The 'natural' setting suggests that, despite the formal attire, grief is a wild and uncontrollable emotion. Private collection. • 1 5 4

26. European buttons decorate a black, scarlet and indigo embroidered ceremonial dress, early twentieth century, and as with many traditional costumes the buttons are purely decorative. Courtesy of Zandra Rhodes. • 1 6 0

27. This flattened rice cake-like ivory *manju* netsuke, decorated with the carved figure of Princess Wakana, gaining spiritual powers from a spider spirit. By Reigyoku, Japan 1859–1900. V&A (564-1904). • 1 6 3

28. Lapland and Iceland, so remote that though this exquisite button is probably eighteenth or nineteenth century, it remains

LIST OF PLATES

Plate 1. *Shroud for a Colourful Soul*, Jane Burch Cochran, 44" × 66", 2005. Materials: fabrics, bullion beads, sequins, paint, found crotched items, gloves and buttons. Method: hand appliquéd quilted and embellished, machine patchwork and hand tied using buttons.

Plate 2. One of Grayson Perry's fabulous *Claires*, the blue ceramic 'crucifixion' buttons made to go with a skirt decorated with a face of Jesus design.

Plate 3. *Ovuliidae*, map of Paris, signed and sealed, Elisabeth Lecourt. A smart girl's dress fashioned from a map and buttoned up as it should be, 2008.

Plate 4. *Tea for Two*, a textile three-dimensional coffee pot, held together – stabbed through – with buttons, by Priscilla Jones. Mixed media with found objects, 2006.

Plate 5. *Mens Suits*, an installation by Charles LeDray, commissioned and produced by Artangel, 2009. Photograph by Julian Abrams.

Plate 6. *Empty Me*, Ran Hwang, 2009, National Museum of Contemporary Art, Korea, 210 × 540 cm (six panels in all). Buttons pinned on wood panel.

Plate 7. Ann Carrington, detail of *Crown Jewels*, the natural mother-of-pearl buttons in all their subtle variety of shape and colour, shown front and back, like a shimmering constellation.

Plate 8. Zandra Rhodes handmade buttons, with her definitive panache: (a) Hand-embroidered covered button edged with satin pleating used on pleated jacket. (b) Queen of Hearts Collection, classic button edged with rhinestones. (c) Hand-embroidered with gold gathered edging used on pleated jacket. (d) Printed and hand-fringed for African Collection.

ACKNOWLEDGEMENTS

The collections of the Victoria and Albert Museum (hereafter V&A) and the Imperial War Museum in London, Waddesdon Manor in Buckinghamshire, the Museum and Art Gallery in Birmingham and the Musée de la Mode in Paris have yielded a wealth of examples. My thanks to the Frick Collection New York for advice on images. I am indebted to Diana Epstein and Millicent Saffro's opulent book *Buttons*; to the bible of the collector's world, *The Big Book of Buttons* by Elizabeth Hughes and Marion Lester; to Martyn Frith of The Button Queen London, Farah Qureshi at the Foundling Museum London, Rachel Boak at Waddesdon and Katy Malone at Atlanta Airport; to the insight of Alison Lurie and to the generous input from collectors at the British Button Society, including Suzanne Barr, Ann Blight, Carey Bromell, Angela Clark, Jenny Curtis, Jan Farrow, Sally Fletcher, Robert White and to Adrian Grater, who lent me books; to the contemporary artists, galleries, commissioning bodies and designers who were prepared to talk and allow their work to be reproduced here (Artangel London, Anita Besson of Galerie Besson London, Judith Brown, Ann Carrington, Ray Caesar, Jane Burch Cochran, Heatherwick Studio London, Michelle Holmes, Ran Hwang, Priscilla Jones, Kate Kessling, Elisabeth Lecourt, Grayson Perry and the Victoria Miro Gallery London, Lucy Quartermaine and Zandra Rhodes); and thanks to Philip Attwood, Karen Bauer, Jill Blythe, Judith Bronkhurst, Alienor de Chambrier, Dan Bee Chung, Josie Floyd, John Good,

Henrietta Harris, Linda Hepner, Mr Huang, Jane Reddish, Munekazu Tanabe, John Vassallo, Dick Vigers, Bo Wang, Derek Wedgwood; special thanks both to Jeremy Edwards for untold computer and photographic services and to Peter Edwards and Oliver Leaman for their many comments and suggestions on early versions of the manuscript; to Philippa Brewster, my editor, who backed this project and for her detailed comments; and thanks to all at I.B. Tauris. Also to the late Malcolm Bowie, my supervisor on an abandoned dissertation on Mallarmé. Without them all I should have made more errors and omissions, but, more than this, they helped keep alive the belief that the button was a worthy, endlessly allusive subject of enquiry.

INTRODUCTION

To set out my stall, I am fond of buttons. One day a friend asked me about my collection, or rather my haphazard clutch of the things. I should like to say that I impressed with my grasp of their historical and socio-economic relevance. Instead, I described how I like to pore over them, run my fingers through them, to sort those I had got round to sewing into sets, those still attached to their original now worn and torn cards. Sometimes I sort them for size, sometimes for colour, smell the fat petrol Bakelite of some, the metal ones like tin foil bitten from a chocolate bar. Some of them, quite a lot of them, are important to me – I associate them with childhood and what can happily be chewed. I began to try to explain why I value them: where this one had been garnered, from the linty pocket of a thrift shop jacket, a disregarded treasure, a tiny painting of dandelions and cornflowers, signifying the passage of time perhaps. The delicate clock seed head seems resonant of some long gone summer meadow, the cornflowers, elliptically sometimes known as bachelor's buttons. Might not they be from some grand old flashy waistcoat, some early eighteenth-century gorgeous toque silk folly – maybe, maybe?

The friend pointed out that, since the button appeared to be made of celluloid, which, though the term was of eighteenth-century origin, was not invented until the latter part of the nineteenth century, and since this example appeared to be more twentieth century, then this was somewhat unlikely. I hurried on, about the way fragments of a pale blue Clydella shirt still adhered to another (Peter Jones, the London store, and my school); a fragment of ointment pink elastic, half melted to a garter button by some iron long ago, causing the bland little face to grimace comically, trailing a ratty gingham ribbon flapper's turban in faded, patriotic post-First World War red, white and blue and the beginning of a story my grandmother told of her heyday when she had had three fiancés simultaneously; the corded cream and gold stuff covered with diamanté studded ones on a strapless cocktail dress, from the photograph of my parents, smiling, glamorous, smoking, before the 1960s had fossilized my mother's sense of style.

At first he seemed mystified, even a little scornful, and I began to regret revealing another private foible. Then he mentioned the large coat button he kept in his saucer of spare change; that sometimes he polished it, with a touch of shaving oil, as it tended to pick up dust, and in fact he suspected it might well be made of casein, pointing out a striated effect along the edge, brown on deeper brown, and that this casein was derived from a protein found in cow's milk, and particularly popular in Italy in the late 1940s or thereabouts. Apparently he had happened to notice it, hanging on a loose thread, when he was bagging up his father's overcoat, and that somehow he had not liked to throw it out. Here was someone male and thoroughly grown up who had, I imagined, been trawling the Internet for information on a single, nondescript button.

A button you would find in any common or garden tin, any charity shop, lying forgotten on the floor, clogging a gutter, just part of the silt and waste of life. He admitted taking pleasure in a growing collection of tiny self-seal plastic bags which housed solitary shirt buttons and that somehow he could not part with them, even though the garments they were intended for had long since been used to wipe oil from a dipstick, or something equally manly. I began to have my doubts about him. What sort of anorak was this? But I wrenched my feminist self back into play. If he could be interested, then it seemed to me anyone could, and I realized I did not know half enough about the button.

> And with a bend of gold tasseled
> And knoppis fyne of gold enameled...
> (knoppis: ornamental buttons)

> (Geoffrey Chaucer, *The Romaunt of the Rose*, c.1370,
> ll. 1069–70)

Buttons can be things of rare beauty. This book is about fashion, through the vehicle of the button, in its narrowest and its widest sense, *on the button* of its pervasive influence. Fashion and the button are intimately caught up together and so to begin to grasp how and why the button develops as it does there is a need to consider fashion more broadly. In the modern-day, post-eighteenth-century fashion machine the button plays a pivotal role, feeding its rapacious appetite in cycles of consumer desire. In the West at least, we are immersed in fashion. Linda Grant is right in *The Thoughtful Dresser* to talk of fashion as an idea in the imagination of the designer, long before the clothes themselves come into existence. In ordinary daydreams,

1. *One Ruby Button*, Kate Kessling, 2008.

too, we can become the different personae imagined clothes make of us: sleek and confident, clothed in charm. Clothes dress our bodies, but they also may reveal – whether we like it or not – our concerns about ourselves and the world.

Old clothes can seem invested with memory. Wardrobes of familiar but discarded garments groan with the past; even a stud button forgotten at the back of a drawer can seem to haunt. To wear something that once belonged to someone now missing, or even a garment that they once admired, can feel tenderly intimate. In contrast, having to wear costume, in the theatre say, previously worn by someone else, bearing the traces of their sweat, worn in the places where it has rubbed against their body, the buttonholes pulled in the places another body has required, can feel complicated and distracting. Clothes and their buttons can seem inhabited by another. You know you are in love when the sight of a button about to come loose on their jacket catches you out in desire; just as surely the spell is broken when a would-be jolly unbuttoning elicits nothing but regret. Actors may rely on finding the right clothes to complete their notion of a character, but clothes can just as easily get in the way. My grandmother, a notably keen but poor needlewoman, is still present in the replaced buttons on a cardigan she must once have mended for my mother, for sewn on with such ferocious diligence, in a slightly wrongly coloured wool that has become twisted and thickened in the wash, I can revisit the course of her arthritic fingers as they pulled each shank too tight.

After all, it may be no coincidence that all but the fabric – the thread, zip, trimmings and of course the buttons, are traditionally listed on the back of *Vogue* and *Simplicity* sewing patterns under the heading NOTIONS, and in Butterick patterns, until recently, NOTIONS NEEDED. Buttons become an exemplar of the notion or idea of fashion. Just as those buttons of the nineteenth century, which once housed cotton swatches soaked in perfume, may still retain a lingering trace of scent, so all buttons can yield, on close attention, a residue of their past, revealing secrets of their former life. I think this plays a large part in why we find ourselves fond of them at times – why they seem significant over and above their function.

This book is about the button – about the button's relation to other fastenings, and later, in Chapter 10, about the development of the American button-badge, its uses as a political symbol and the virtual button. But while I tackle something of the tin and bone, plastic and glass actuality, I also want to sift out the flotsam, the imaginative undertow that even so small an object may throw up in its wake. Hans Anderson's Emperor is not entirely wrong to value his new clothes because they are imaginary. He may realize that the splendid, tasteful, enhancing, perfectly fitting and perfectly buttoned clothes cannot ever exist, for the perfect form has to remain in the realm of aspiration, forever beyond his grasp. As the cavaliers hold up the notional train of exquisite fabric, I see the pink and pampered flesh wobbling along with head held bravely high, walking a little faster perhaps as that brat cries out 'But he has nothing on!' Buttons have come to have an existence in our imaginations too.

Clothes designers might choose their buttons with care, yet in Britain at least, where fabrics have traditionally been more dominant, they can play a more subordinate role. In many of the great European fashion houses, however, the choice of buttons is still considered an integral part of a designer's work. In Chapter 5, I will be looking at the role of the trademark in the history of the button.

Elsa Schiaparelli is a designer who was fascinated by fastenings, and during the 1920s and 1930s cast buttons in all manner of whimsical and trompe l'oeil shapes (see Chapter 5). However, she seems to have drawn away from the button, becoming fascinated by the possibilities of the zip and other innovative fastenings. Of her 1934 collection, *Time Magazine* declared: 'Mme Elsa Schiaparelli ... glorifies the gadget, persecutes the button'. In the fickle dance of fashion the button cannot always seem of the moment, but again and again it returns to the limelight of style.

It is no accident that the word fashion has commonly been used to describe the way we behave, in one fashion or another, 'after a fashion', 'in a similar fashion', 'the fashion of the times' and so on. Fashion has come to refer to the way we dress and more particularly our style of dress, but this underlying sense of moral behaviour remains lurking and can lend a certain disapproval to the way many feel they should view fashion. In literature, fashion is often treated with disdain, and sometimes this opprobrium attaches itself to the button. Buttons may seem not just vulgarly showy, but to betray a vulgarity of intent (Chapters 4 and 8). However, in contrast, in Jane Austen's *Emma*, when Emma contrives to find out if Mr Knightley is considering Jane Fairfax romantically, buttons both betray his real affections to the reader and come to his aid by concealing his distress from Emma herself:

> Mr Knightley was hard at work upon the lower buttons of his thick leather gaiters, and either the exertion of getting them together, or some other cause, brought the colour into his face...

> (Jane Austen, *Emma*, 1815, ch. 33)

Here the gaiters seem to represent his morally depend-able (but compared with the dashing Henry Crawford) unexciting character; the buttons provide a refuge, the simple task of buttoning masking his emotion.

There are many such examples for the choices people make about their dress – once such choices were made possible by affordability and access – for they are com-pletely embedded in our post-Enlightenment value judge-ments about each other. The button acts as a microcosm, a very Tardis of potential meaning, like a single stalwart person standing for the universe of fashion.

No, no Peter! No *buttons*. No thimbles.

(Older Wendy to Peter Pan)

But why the button and not some more worthy accou-trement – something with a little more gravitas attached, perhaps? Cannot much the same be said of the buckle, the hook or the belt – and yet they do not seem to carry the same air of comedy about them? Chocolate buttons by any other name might not seem so sweet, and Harpo chooses to eats the buttons and not another part of a bellboy's waistcoat, in the Marx Brothers' *The Cocoanuts* (1929). It might be possible to conjugate any detail of dress in much the same way, though it would not have, as we shall see, the same historical and cultural pedigree as the button. The literature of the zip may be more con-temporary and pleasingly brutal (Chapters 8 and 10), but it seems to lack a certain pathos. Unlike the button it promises more than it delivers – all teeth and no lips.

There is something about the button that demands our affections. The Internet is full of bloggers claiming to love them: buttons themselves, American button-badges, paper buttons for craftwork, button jewellery, button print textiles, bellybuttons... The button seems to key enthusiasm. From the many pages of sites for the button there is: 'Don't resist this urge, it's a healthy hobby and good for your nostalgia button' (www.antiquebuttoncollecting.com); 'It's my Nan's fault. She got us all hooked, ha! My wife left me. Said it was her or buttons – I love my buttons' (www.myspace); or perhaps, from the buttonfloozies.blogspot.com, simple or possibly sinister, 'I love to stare at buttons'.

Button societies thrive. Button collections, be they ever so humble, are seldom lightly discarded. In the Brazilian film *Caixa de Botões*, the titular box of buttons acts as a symbol of the teenage protagonist's learning to forgive the past. Look button tins up on eBay and you will find that the sellers, wary of seeming callous about so tender a fetish, will talk of them as having been greatly valued and sadly offered to the market, retro or vintage rather than merely old, as if looking for a new home for a much loved pet for whom the owner can no longer care. It is implied that their value lies not merely in the buttons themselves but in the connection one can make with the previous owner's ancestor, say, or more mysterious estate sale, and like any self-respecting orphan of the romantic school, the unknown parentage is usually assumed to be grand. Even a mildly cynical selling ploy can begin to reveal the connotations that have evolved around the button.

Literature and history support this sense of peculiar value. The Amish find them too showy. In Peter Weir's 1985 film *Witness* the young Amish woman Rachel attempts to conceal the detective John Book's identity by lending him her deceased husband's clothes:

Rachel: I should tell you this kind of coat doesn't have buttons. See? Hooks and eyes.
John: Something wrong with buttons?
Rachel: Buttons are proud and vain, not plain.
John: Got anything against zippers?

This is elegant, succinct scriptwriting: ethics, sex and their burgeoning intimacy, and all through the vehicle of the button. Elizabeth I adopted buttons to transcend male power. At a time when those of any consequence were principally worn by men, Elizabeth gloried in the expense and display of her many exquisite sets of buttons, perhaps influenced by and determined to match the splendour of visiting Spanish emissaries or portraits of Philip II of Spain himself. Renaissance women might hold elaborate masks in place by sucking on a button in each corner of their mouths. Napoleon's armies were defeated by tin buttons that crumbled and fell away in the Russian winter, leaving the poor French soldiers to freeze; George 'Beau' Brummell thought them better discreet; Louis XIV spent fortunes on their acquisition, whereas for Beatrix Potter's Tailor of Gloucester, almost defeated by a lack of cherry-coloured silk for the one-and-twenty buttonholes required for the mayor's wedding coat, they are exquisitely sewn by a team of mice, and success and contentment ensue.

Buttons can act as watches, as *memento mori*, as romantic lockets, as places for hiding poison, for concealing contraband, as compasses, James Bond cameras or to deter soldiers (some say sailors) from wiping their noses on their cuffs, a use credited variously to Elizabeth I, King Frederick the Great of Prussia and Napoleon Bonaparte. A button can be a paltry thing, of humble purpose, apparently insignificant, cheaply got, easily lost and replaced – yet boasts its own profession, its own taxes, and impassioned collectors seek out precious finds in gold, silver, precious jewels, involving the best, most innovative craft techniques. The button can be transformed into great art, but even in its most modest form it can carry a weight of symbolic significance. It can seem imbued with memory and longing for the lost past. It can stand for grief or represent a totalitarian regime.

The button, in its impact on clothes and its relation to fashion, is a vanguard on the battleground of gender issues and in the context of Thorstein Veblen's theory of conspicuous consumption where, for example, shifts in who wears showy buttons demonstrate the ways in which status and power are portrayed and developed. As Quentin Bell argues for the morality of clothes in general, so the modest button is as useful in our understanding of humanity as the fruit fly is to the science of genetics:

the study of clothes is of capital importance in any consideration of human behaviour

(Quentin Bell, *On Human Finery*, 1976, p. 16)

It is in this context that the button – small, portable, changing and responding, punching way above its weight – takes on meaning for the student of human nature, its development and attitudes to it and the ways we have come to speak of it, acting as a touchstone of our values.

Buttons form a link between the applied arts and the great aesthetic movements. Despite sometimes being of little financial value, the button has often relied on great skill in its production. Buttons reflect cultural changes and technological and industrial developments. Often collectors have related how much it is the difficulty of determining the make-up of button finds that has led them to further study and discovery. Buttons have been a means of liberal education, in fact. From ancient Egyptian scarabs and the finds of Herculaneum and Pompeii there is evidence of decorative buttons of a sort, and in the mid-thirteenth century Étienne Boileau's *Mastery of Trades* documents the separation of button making into its own category, rather than coming under the governance of jewellers' or tailors' guilds. Diderot required eight pages to do them and button makers justice in his *Encyclopédie* of 1745, demonstrating the importance of the button in sumptuous dress. In the extraordinary archaeological discovery of the *Mary Rose* in 1966 – a warship of Henry VIII of England which sank in 1545 – were identified not only simple buttons made of wool, silk and leather but also sets of fine ornate buttons, spherical, hemispherical, pear-shaped and covered in green or crimson silk. Sumptuary legislation in Europe and colonial America in the seventeenth century betrays the growing significance of the button. Before the eighteenth century clothes tended to denote rank, but in Europe, from the Age of the Enlightenment, emerged the idea of fashion as we know it, as something unstable, ephemeral and accessible to anyone – albeit still a tiny minority of society at large – who can afford it. The button demonstrates this fundamental shift.

This history of the button will be explored in Chapters 3 and 4, and I will draw on a range of anecdotes to make my case; but I begin with some more personal disparate images: my grandfather, best-dressed man in Leicester for three years no less, the epitome of elegance to us, owned but three suits all his life. They had plain brown buttons. I sat on his knee playing the laughing farmer and trying to grasp them as I trotted on; my mother's wedding dress

2. Wedding 1948 and dress. The buttons run down the back and up each Rapunzel sleeve.

3. A tin for buttons and other small discarded things.

in duchesse satin, grown crisp with age at the bottom of a wardrobe, rows of tiny covered buttons run all down the back and up each sleeve, Rapunzel-style. Several of them have worn away from their metal shank; my father, awkward in his army dress uniform, fat gilt buttons glinting in the light from the landing as he kisses me goodnight, his cheek damp and smelling of Knight's Castile soap; I inherit from my grandmother her button tin. Treasure: there are beige army shirt buttons, Air Force buttons still attached to squares of uniform fabric from an uncle whose Wellington was shot down on his first mission in December 1940, horn overcoat buttons, leather plaited buns, tiny mother-of-pearl, linen-covered and two from my mother's wedding dress, stained with rust like old blood. Like all such tins, other items that could not easily be discarded have collected there over the years. I find a gob-stopper marble, various beads, a bodkin, a Silver Jubilee crown, the broken head of a clay pipe in the form of a veiled lady, a Sacred Heart medal, a nutmeg, a sewing machine part and a small-sized base metal wedding ring – all unexplained but evidently of value once, but with nowhere else to go.

Buttons inhabit this world of small things, often no longer of use, with which we once came into daily intimate contact and that knowledge imbues old buttons with a certain potency. Though the word button can denote something of no value, as in 'not worth a button', one can be 'worth a button or two' or 'cute as a button', 'button lovely' or even 'on the button'.

I am not a true collector and in Chapter 2 I ask why some people collect, and collect buttons in particular. I have been able to draw on the scholarship of collectors and historians, the curators and designers, novelists, poets, artists, potters, quilters, philosophers of fashion, of anthropology, television and film-makers who have illuminated the subject – not to mention the host of stories that reveal the true complex nature of buttons and button-ness.

The following chapters map the development of and discuss the ways in which cultural change has affected our attitudes to the button. But, first of all, I ask what buttons are and what are they for. After Alison Lurie's *The Language of Clothes*, I want to conjugate buttons to find out what they can reveal about ourselves – what impact the button has on our language and, in turn, discover what this shows up about our attitudes to the button.

CHAPTER ONE

As a Notion

I believe in the total depravity of inanimate things...
the elusiveness of soap, the knottiness of string,
the transitory nature of buttons.

(Katherine Walker, *The Atlantic Monthly*,
1864, vol. 14, p. 361)

Buttons are surprisingly elusive. They have entered so deep into the imagination that it is easy to lose sight of their ordinary actuality. Yet buttons are, quite simply, something for fastening two pieces of fabric together, usually in the form of a small disc or knob that passes through a buttonhole or loop. The word derives from the French *bouton*, which means bud – suggesting something living, pregnant with potential growth, something almost imperceptible from which much may follow and without which something would never have come into existence. *Bouton* itself derives from the Old French *boton*, from *boter*, meaning to thrust. So the word 'button' also implies something that bears fruit or flowers, and, supposing the button thrusts its way through said buttonhole or loop, it becomes, in a sense, dynamic, with the implication that it has something of a will of its own. Significantly, buttons are a European feature of dress. The verb 'to button' was not used until the thirteenth century, which suggests that by then the button itself had come to be more significant, more highly valued. Whatever the noun, it requires a verb to bring it alive, to form a sentence that can express meaning. Just as they recall the past, buttons can drive us forward into the future.

Whereas the Italian *bottone*, Spanish *botón* and Portuguese *botão* share the same linguistic root, in much of the rest of northern Europe the equivalent word stems from the German word, *Knopf*: hence the Danish *knap*, Dutch *knoop*, Finnish *nappi*, Norwegian and Swedish *knapp*. In Middle Low German, *Knobbe* is a knot in wood, and in Middle Dutch *cnoppe* is a bud. Yet the Old French *boter* itself has Germanic origins. Most of the words for button in Europe are closely related to each other.

It is worth mentioning here that in German there are a host of button-related slang expressions relating to money. The Russian *knopka* again may suggest a knob or bud. In China, *niu kou* has no such connotation and reinforces the country's long non-European tradition of fabric and loop buttons; European influence is evident, however, in the Japanese *botan*, because the word does not exist in kanji (and so is not derived from the Chinese language), the implication being that such words were introduced during the Meiji Restoration period (1868–1912) after over 250 years of self-imposed isolation. In many non-European countries the word for button is also a term for buckle, brooch or clamp, as with the Latin *fibula*. When buttons arrived on the scene pre-existing terms were often adapted for their use, so, since they were bud-like, nob-ish, our

European linguistic terms were adopted, even if something of their derivation remains. The button can seem full of potential organic life.

One reason for a pre-thirteenth century absence of verbal punch in the noun-only use of the word 'button' may be because early buttons were not functional, but seem to have been used solely for ornament. Most early medieval clothes consisted of un-stitched fabric wrapped about the body and held in place by sashes, belts or brooches, as is still the case in many more traditional cultures. Contemporary buttonless fashion, as, for example, in many of the asymmetric designs of the fashion designer Issey Miyake, or the oversized tabards of Sarah Pacini, draws on a connection with a sense of primordial dress, and in this context buttons speak of the modern. There is no definite evidence for verifying that what appear to be early buttons, from, say, the Indus Valley Civilization of ancient Pakistan, 2800–2600 BC, were ever used to button, since the garments they may have once been attached to have long since rotted away. The pre-history department of the British Museum advise that nothing that could be called a button exists in the older collections. Fur and leather clothing was probably laced rather than buttoned, or toggled together during the Palaeolithic and Mesolithic periods. It is possible that the earliest buttons were found in Egypt and date from about 2000 BC; they are recognized as buttons because there is a means of sewing them onto fabric, with a hole or holes, or signs of loop or shank. Some buttons are fixed permanently but nonetheless hold two pieces of fabric together, as in quilting. It is likely that the buttonhole had yet to be invented, which one might argue precluded any need for buttoning – although fastening loops predate the buttonhole. Tribes in the Amazon forests still embellish their minimal clothes with sewn-on stones and carved wood and bone, which suggests that the urge to adorn ourselves is deeply rooted and that the button emerges from this fundamental desire.

The earliest functioning buttons may be inferred from later centuries' less highly valued examples, such as those simply made by gathering together a piece of cloth (see Chapter 10), with the raw edges tucked in to form the stuffing and a shank formed from the remaining thread. Such easily made items, often produced from off-cuts and requiring little skill in their making, were later, and usually unsuccessfully, legislated against as injurious to the professional button makers' trade. *The Parliamentary Gazetteer of England and Wales* reports measures taken in support of a bill in 1778 intended to stop such 'silk, mohair and twist' trade in Macclesfield:

> Buttons covered with garment stuffs being proscribed and informers actually set upon the watch to denounce them, horn and metal buttons soon began to show their polished faces.

(*The Parliamentary Gazetteer*, 1778, vol. 3, p. 331)

However, until cheap machine-made buttons became widely available, fabric buttons were largely the only sort of button available to the poor, apart from those gained from hand-me-downs from the rich or on uniforms provided by employers. Homemade buttons include the crotched button and the English Dorset thread button, which was originally made in that county alone in the mid-eighteenth century and would have offered a supplementary trade for lacemakers. It was made by weaving threads and sometimes wool over a metal ring in a cartwheel design. Interestingly, the word 'nubbin', for an underdeveloped ear of maize or other vegetable, is also a term for the loose threads that might be used to stuff a fabric button, and in turn it stems from a nub or small rounded object, like a button.

In the 1840s homemade buttons were largely superseded by the linen three-fold button, which was patented in 1841 by the Birmingham manufacturer John Aston. This button achieved a flatter and more uniform finish. Three layers of linen in varying degrees of fineness were wrapped around a pasteboard mould and held in place by a circle of metal, all the raw edges being sandwiched within. Such buttons were popular in underwear, particularly as the coarser linen formed a shank that was more comfortable for the wearer than metal.

Charles Dickens was fascinated by the Birmingham button manufacturing processes and in his weekly journal describes, with the optimism of the age, how the three-fold is made, in contrast to the previous hand-covered method:

> Some grandmothers…may remember…horn button moulds by the string, to be covered at home. Some middle-aged ladies may remember the anxieties of the first attempts to cover such moulds – one of the most important lessons given to the infant needlewoman…how many stitches…What coaxing to stretch the cover smooth! What danger of unraveling…what ruin if the thread broke!…And now, by two turns of a handle, the covering is done to such perfection that the button will last twice as long as of old, and dozens can be covered in a minute by one woman.

And in a happy image he describes this new convenience:

> it is as great a mystery where the edges are all put away,
> as how the apple gets into the dumpling.

(Charles Dickens, *Household Words*, 1852,
vol. 5, p. 109)

Just why the button began to be used is harder to discover, but it seems likely that it not only made it possible for clothes to fit more snugly, allowing for convenience and warmth, avoiding the discomfort of sharp pins and hooks, but also for a more figure-hugging and potentially flattering, corset-like effect. The philosopher Arthur Schopenhauer recommends recourse to such flattering clothing, to 'cover up the insignificance or ugliness of his person under barbaric finery'.[1] Buttons can also enable a person to dress or undress easily and quickly, although in practice the more affluent reversed this possible advantage by making it a feature of rich dress that the buttons are often tiny and numerous, and thus time-consuming and difficult to manage without help. Not for nothing does the traditional white bridal gown often have rows of tiny buttons, representing the notion of the virgin modestly revealing herself, button by button, on her wedding night.

In the eleventh and twelfth centuries the Crusaders carried home to Europe buttoned garments from Palestine, from their encounters with Turks and Mongols, and so began a European obsession with the button, with buttoned sleeves and front openings, allowing us to develop their use in order to display the human form, and for the idea of that tightness, shape and function to begin to invade our language.

If buttons are part of the vocabulary of dress, Alison Lurie, in *The Language of Clothes*, suggests that, along with other details of dress, they might be seen to perform the role of qualifying adjectives or adverbs, with the implication that they are not as important as the nouns and verbs of her figurative sentences of dress.[2] Sometimes buttons could be said to play a pivotal role in the sentence of someone's apparel. One is forced back to the actuality of clothes, where a garment that has lost even one of its buttons can seem ruined, which is not generally the case were an adjective or adverb to be removed from a sentence.

Buttons have survived the caprices of fashion, whereas gloves and hats are nowadays relatively marginalized. The beanie, sun-hat or cold-weather gloves aside, it is rare for these items to be worn other than on formal occasions. One might say that a particular hat finishes off an ensemble, making it seem more complete, but a missing button on a lounge suit can seem to wholly negate the formal, smart effect, making the wearer seem not a real suit-type, businesslike type of person. Partly this is because even when their function has died out, as with the buttons on the sleeves of conventional men's jackets, or those that once buttoned back the trailing coat tails of the seventeenth- and eighteenth-century gentleman to enable him to more easily mount a horse, their vestigial presence can make a garment seem right and finished. When they are missing, the intention of the suit is subverted. Missing buttons, even when they have not fulfilled a function when present, can make someone seem uncared for, and suggest perhaps a fall from prosperity, like the derelict playing his violin in the street, still elegant in tie and tails, but betrayed by the missing buttons of his jacket.

4. Buttons tend to come in sets. *Diamond*, Kate Kessling, 2008.

Moreover, buttons tend to come in sets. One might have a jacket with only one button, but generally we are accustomed to seeing at least three, usually in an ordered matching row down the front of a shirt, jacket or coat. Cuffs may have only one button, or more, but the other sleeve must match them. Even outré, non-symmetric fashions, where sleeves are designed with quite different shapes, say, rely on subverting a sense of the expected, mirror-imaged set. There are various 'rules' that have developed about how one should or should not button. I was always schooled that no gentleman ever buttoned any but the central button of a jacket. There is more general consensus about always leaving one's bottom button undone, if not for fashion, then certainly for comfort, as in the old music hall song:

> I can't do my bally bottom button up…
> (bally: euphemism for bloody)
> And it's so tight and it serves me right,
> Must have eaten too much grub last night,
> I can't do my bally bottom button up,
> And though you think it's fun,
> What's the use of buttoning the other bally buttons,
> When the bally bottom button's undone.

> (Written and composed by J. P. Long,
> sung by Ernie Mayne, 1904)

This may refer to waistcoat buttons, where such a sartorial rule stands for all but shorter, more square-cut styles.

We are drawn to patterning. For example, a full, reasonably even set of teeth is required, aesthetically speaking, though an off-centre glint of gold or inset diamond may be felt to enhance. Stamp collectors seek out missing stamps to complete their sets. A brother of mine acquired for very little outlay all but one of a set of William Nicholson engravings: had it been complete, it would have been worth a great sum. A much-repeated family tale involves an elderly relative quietly remonstrating, without irony, in defence of a one-eyed acquaintance, 'Oh, but she has such a lovely eye!' Indeed where sets are incomplete, it is not uncommon for the collector to keep just one and sell off the rest, so unsatisfactory is the imperfect set.

The artist Joseph Beuys plays on an expectation of what should be present in his work *Felt Suit* (1970). We see a plain, grey man's two-piece, but there is something odd about it. The felt allows for no fine detail, all is matt, and there are no buttons. No buttonholes. All he allows are two plain pocket flaps and the zigzag of the lapels. Beuys used felt in previous work, and we shall later be looking at the poignancy of the collection in relation to the Holocaust and the recycling of both buttons and of hair and fat into felt. However, it is the absence of buttons here that is important. Beuys said once that he had omitted 'mere trifles', yet in doing so he is better drawing attention to them. He claimed 'if somebody wants to wear the suit, he can fasten it with safety pins', or in other words make do, safety pins being of their nature temporary stop-gaps, things that are not permanently intended to fasten a garment. When pressed to give reasons for using felt, he says that it is because it is not smart, with no further explanation.

It is not for the artist to press the significance of his or her work. There seems to be some relation between Beuys's suit and the idea of a convict's uniform, with all fastenings removed, yet Beuys rejects this interpretation, claiming it is more the case that 'one has to omit mere trifles, such as complicated buttons ... (felt) isn't suited for buttonholes and the like' (interview with Jörg Schellman and Bernd Klüser, 1970). Conversely, Beuys admits that his buttonless suit cannot help but bring a prisoner to mind. Is the lack of buttons to deny the convict a better sense of identity, of feeling appropriately dressed, or might it be that their absence tokens disgrace, as with the court-marshalled soldier, being ritually stripped of his or her rank? Significantly, in the last 20 years prison garb, particularly in the USA, has tended to use buttonless surgical-type scrubs, such as the orange slops worn by Guantanamo Bay detainees.

The skilled designer will have a feel for choosing buttons. A friend was recently trying to replace a beautiful single button missing from a Betty Jackson jacket of the early 1980s. She was supplied with a telephone number, and, assuming it to be the company offices, found herself put straight through to Jackson herself at home, who, on having the item described, rifled through her personal button tin and was able to replace the missing button. Button sellers delight in the organization of their wares, from the serious in the novel *Thérèse Raquin* where 'black buttons (are) sewn on white card, boxes of all sizes and colours' (Émile Zola, 1867, ch. 1), to the more ebullient as in the real-life self-styled 'button Nazi', Shirley Savoy, who has sold buttons at F&S Fabrics in Los Angeles for many years, rigorously advising customers on what they should and should not choose from her stacks of boxes, 'their sample ends facing out, forming a mad mosaic' (*LA Times*, 18 August 2004). At some level the associations we have with different materials are an essential part of this ability and guide a sophisticated sense of taste.

Almost every substance known to man has at some time been used to make buttons, including all manner of natural solids – woods, nutshells, marbles, slate, corals, bone, horn, amber, sea shells, ivory, pearls, rubber, cork, lava, dogs' teeth, fossilized walrus tusk – as well as glass, metals, plastics, vegetables, enamels, papier mâché, lacquer, paper, cork and butterflies' wings. Fashion often plays with surprising juxtaposition as much as with what seems appropriate, so that whilst a tiny doll-sized mother-of-pearl button can seem right for silk satin or chiffon, a leather knob or even wooden toggle can create a pleasing contrast: finely woven, slippery, feather-light, vulnerable and expensive fabric suggests young skin, sensuality, luxury; leather can evoke tough animal hide, and thus strength and vigour, and wood may bring to mind the rural, natural world. Put them together and one notices. Designers like John Galliano subvert our expectations, draw on complex association, so that a button more suited to a chunky tweed, when discovered on an evening fabric, may also evoke something of 'the rough male kiss of blankets' (Rupert Brooke, 'The Great Lover', 1914), of the masculine and dangerous even, piercing the frail cloth. I am reminded of film starlets of the 1940s and 1950s in chiffon blouses buttoned apparently primly to the neck, yet with their too-heavy glass buttons dragging the flimsy fabric against the upholstered breasts beneath.

Neil Gaiman's cult children's novel *Coraline* (2002), recently made into a 3-D film by director Henry Selick (2009), involves a young girl who moves with her parents into a flat in a sinister old house. There, through a door in their living room, she discovers a parallel world, much as in *Through the Looking Glass*, where everything is the same yet not the same. Her alternative parents are indulgent, giving her cake and the attention she has longed for, but

there is something odd about them: they and all the people on this other side have buttons in place of eyes. They
stare unfeelingly back like the three enormous dogs in the
Hans Christian Anderson story 'The Tinder Box' or the
'shaggy dogs with buttons instead of eyes' in the Russian
folk tale 'The Golden Key'. If this is the world of the child's
id, then the eyes are the gateways, and such windows to
what should be the soul disclose only a black, blank button stare.

The terror Coraline comes to experience implies
koumpounophobia, or a pathological fear of buttons. This
is a fairly common condition, but sufferers are wary of
derision, a fear of buttons apparently not having the same
solemnity that attaches to other more openly admitted
phobias. In early 2010 Penny Leaver Green designed an
exhibition called *Buttons' Phobia* in Bristol. Think of your
acquaintances and what they wear: perhaps one of them
is always in T-shirts? A nurse claims that she has to wear
gloves when buttoning patients' clothes, such is her panic.
As with most irrational fears, some traumatic event in
early childhood is thought to be the cause, though sufferers often claim they have experienced it for as long as they
can remember and may feel the same response towards
similarly shaped objects, like coins or tiddlywinks. Some
say the very thought of buttons makes them queasy: they
feel they need to wash their hands if they have inadvertently touched one, becoming short of breath, their
heartbeat raised. In the London *Metro* newspaper a suf-
ferer, Gillian Linkins, admits, 'For me touching a button
would be like touching a cockroach, it feels dirty, nasty
and wrong' (London *Metro*, 20 April 2008). For others
the phobia means merely preferring not to wear buttons
and avoiding focusing on others' buttons. Some say plastic

buttons are more disturbing than metal or that those with four holes are more alarming than ones with only two. In the illustrations for *Coraline* and in the animated film, the black eyes of the alternative beings appropriately have four blank holes.

It is significant that buttons turn up regularly in folk tales and children's stories, suggesting that even to a child they hold ambiguous value. Pinocchio hopes to buy his carpenter father a coat with diamond buttons in *The Adventures of Pinocchio* by Carlo Collodi, and in 'The Gingerbread Man', by Paul Galdone, there is pathos in the lonely old woman who, yearning to make her biscuit companion seem human, 'puts a row of raisins down the front of his jacket for buttons'. In 'The Ebony Horse' in *The Arabian Nights*, the animal carries the Prince through the sky, with one button-switch for increasing and decreasing speed, and another for flying up and down. In Grimm's 'Frederick and Catherine', Kate digs up gold coins from her garden, but, mistaking them for worthless yellow buttons, she exchanges them with a peddler for earthenware dishes. Oscar Wilde's *The Happy Prince*, has Hans forced to sell the silver buttons from his coat during a hard winter. The *Uncle Remus* stories by Joel Chandler Harris (1845), said to be of African or American Cherokee origin, and later adapted by Enid Blyton, has Br'er Fox using buttons for the Tar Baby's eyes, to entrap Br'er Rabbit in a sticky briar-patch situation.

The word 'button' also occurs as a name for geographical locations, as in Button Island, in Hingham Massachusetts and Button Valley City, Montana, in the United States, which are named, like South Button Island in the Andaman and Nicobar Islands off the coast of India, to suggest their small size; the word is also not an uncommon name for roads, streets and avenues and establishments such as the coffee house frequented by Hogarth in the 1730s; and as a proper name, as in Jenson Button, the British Formula One racing car driver, Dick Button, the American figure skater of the 1940s and 1950s, Button Gwinnet, one of the signatures of the American Declaration of Independence, and the comedian Red Buttons, who hosted his own television show in the 1950s and lately had a recurring role in *ER*, the television drama. Red Buttons's surname stems from a nickname, since he had worked as a hotel porter as a young man. It was the lavish livery of menservants, or 'button boys', that also gave rise to the name of Buttons for the flunky in the pantomime *Cinderella*. The film *COPS* (1988) had a character bombastically nicknamed Buttons McBoom Boom. In F. Scott Fitzgerald's short story 'The Curious Case of Benjamin Button' (1921), later made into a film of the same name (2008), the father of the reverse-ageing hero owns a button factory. *Button Moon* was the name of a 1980s ITV children's television programme, set in a land where kitchen utensils came to life, and in each episode Mr Spoon would travel in his space rocket to a large silvery button in a blanket sky, a place of mystery and adventure. The hell-raiser rock band F*ck Buttons terms its band members as the Buttons. A decoy in an auction room, whose job it is to trick the unwary into bidding, was once known as a button: one who buttons up or entraps their marks. The centre of the target in the Scottish game of curling is called house, or the button.

An avalanche of metaphors springs from the button: 'to button your lip' is to keep quiet; someone who is 'buttoned up' is thought to be inhibited, passionless or taciturn; if you are 'unbuttoned', you are uninhibited or unrestrained. It may be worth noting here, however, that a similar metaphorical

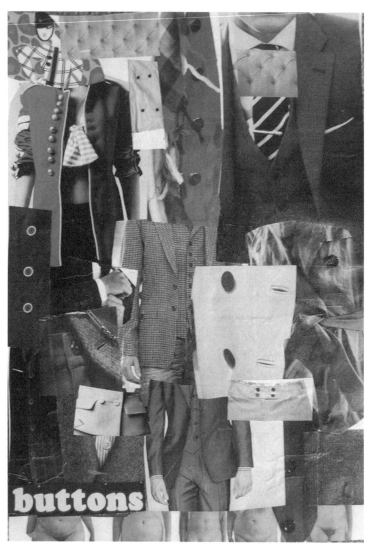

5. Nellie Collier, *Buttons*, 2009.

use of 'unveiled' and 'unzipped' has rather different connotations. Someone who is unzipped is more than unrestrained, bordering on the manic. Historically 'unveiled' suggests something far subtler, more gradual, and perhaps exposing something less shocking, more wonderful.

A button on a cap may be a mark of privilege. In China, for example, it was a symbol of literary achievement, and was consequently adopted in some British public schools, particularly for sporting activities. Mandarins wore different coloured buttons on their silk caps to designate their relative status.

Lurie makes the point that someone usually neatly buttoned makes far greater an impact if found unbuttoned than a habitually untidy person (1981, p. 8). Conversely, to be 'buttoned-down' suggests you are conservative or conventional, as in 'a buttoned-down corporate culture'. To be termed 'a button off' can mean one is unkempt or careless, but if I 'push some serious buttons', I am acutely to the point. In the novel *The Long Goodbye* (1971), Raymond Chandler claims, 'If you press exactly the right buttons and are also lucky, justice may show up in the answer'. A button tow is a type of ski lift for one person, so named because of the circular plate that takes the skier's weight. Cockney rhyming slang pairs button with Len Hutton, the cricketer, and also a leg of mutton, so one might say, 'You need to leg of mutton your Len Huttons'. In contrast, to have a soul above buttons is to be superior to one's lot in life, as in 'My father was an eminent button maker... but I had a soul above buttons... and panted for a liberal profession' (George Colman, *Sylvester Daggerwood*, 1833, act I, scene 1).

Anne Sexton has buttons that will not stay done up inviting ridicule:

Now your beer belly hangs out like Fatso
You are popping your buttons and expelling gas.
How can I lie down with you, my comical beau
When you are so middle-aged and lower-class

(Anne Sexton, 'For Mr Death Who Stands
with his Door Open', 1974)

The human body draws on imagery such as 'bellybut-ton' for navel. The Italian pasta tortellini are known as bellybuttons, a metaphor said to be inspired by a cook's glimpse of Venus's navel through a keyhole. 'Button eyes' are perhaps too small, engaging pinpoints of light or may even be my prosthetic eye, and a 'button nose' is held to be charmingly or possibly too infantile. In Korea it is the holes in a button, or *dan choo*, that are used as an idiom to describe a person with small eyes. In a sexual con-text the word 'button' is used for nipple, as with Nagiko in Peter Greenaway's film *The Pillow Book* (1996), who has 'nipples like bone buttons'. A 'button mushroom' is a slang term for a small penis. The clitoris and anus are sometimes known as buttons, and there is also a more abstract expression for orgasm, in the term 'coming to the button'. More graphically, a 'button buster' is an erection.

Some flowers are so termed. I wear a buttonhole in my lapel, as in Oscar Wilde's *The Importance of Being Earnest* (1895), when Algernon first meets Cecily:

Cecily:... Won't you come in?

Algernon: Thank you. Might I have a buttonhole first? I never have any appetite unless I have a buttonhole first.

Cecily: A Maréchal Niel?

Algernon: No, I'd rather have a pink rose.

(Act II)

In this first encounter Algernon is smitten, so when he prefers a pink rose in this context, the buttonhole becomes both rose and a blushing pink young woman, Cecily herself. In the context of the medieval poem the *Roman de la Rose*, the rosebud is a potent symbol of romantic love, attracting the male eye. As a man bends down close, the arrow fires out of the button/bud and impales him, his curiosity securing his affections.

We eat button mushrooms and chocolate buttons, you may be 'cute as a button', or 'a button short' of the complete set necessary for common sense to reign, but something 'hot button' is politically of the moment and I may delight in your intuition when you 'push my button' or such malicious bullying may provoke me, deliberately encouraging me to react. Pushing the button may mean the nuclear switch, or more generally set off an important chain of events. Moreover, in the United States the button has been borrowed to denote badges, switches on lifts or elevators, computer functions, keypads on mobile phones and so on. I may punch you on the nose or on the button, or the phrase may refer to the chin, as in P. G. Wodehouse's phrase 'He soaked him on the button, don't you know' (*Laughing Gas*, 1936, ch. 2). The end of my scabbard allows me to fence safely with its blunted button; I buttonhole you or *server le bouton* when you would really rather not speak to me but I wouldn't give a button, as in 'I wouldn't care a fig', unless I cared a button for you. The buttonhook is not only a tool used for fastening boots, gaiters or gloves, but American football has adopted the term for a strategic move, where the player doubles back suddenly, as if through a buttonhole.

Botany claims the image for the sycamore tree with its button-like seeds, termed the buttonball tree, and the buttonbush for a low-growing aquatic shrub with globular flower heads. The button fern is an evergreen whose fronds have rounded, button-like pinnae. The buttonwood tree is another word for sycamore again, but it is also used for two types of tropical mangrove, possibly due to the bulbous protuberances of its intertwining aerial roots. In biology button spiders are another name for widow spiders, whose venom can attack the central nervous system: the black button spider is particularly dangerous, its bite causing severe pain; and there is also the less poisonous brown button. Both have globular button-like bodies and comparatively short legs. The button quail is a small quail-like bird, and button buck is a hunter's term for a young male deer whose antlers have not yet developed.

Medical science utilizes both the function and the word for new ways of attaching prosthetic limbs, to click replacement knee caps into place and the tracheotomy button is the end of the plastic tube placed in the stoma to keep it open so that a patient's airway remains unimpeded.

Dental medicine uses buttons to keep false teeth from flipping out, taking advantage of the button's ability to fasten securely whilst allowing for a little movement as with natural teeth, reducing strain on the point of connection and increasing comfort. This need for a hiatus, or room for error between tooth and gum, is comparable to the seamstress needing to allow for movement between button and buttonhole to give an unpuckered, easy fit. There is

AS A NOTION • 21

a general tendency for horizontally placed buttonholes to pull away to the closing edge side, whereas the vertically placed tend to pull in a downward direction. This means that buttonholes have to be placed with this adjustment to the placement line in mind. Some dentists now allow their patients the use of switches, known as dental buttons, with which they can shut off the drill themselves, to make them feel more in control and thus be less anxious.

More than any other current use, the Internet has incorporated the term for its virtual keys or tabs, and we will be returning to the idea of the virtual button in Chapter 10.

> Just so, if one may compare small things with great, an innate love of getting drives these Attic bees each with his own function.

> (Virgil, *Georgics*, IV, l 176)

A button like a bee is small but its influence is great: bees are the great facilitators of plant procreation, the source of honey, and so, to bend a line from *The Duchess of Malfi*, 'to great (buttons) the moral may be stretched'. But what is the point of all these metaphors when button-ness, though so widely used, often does not seem to engage with the function of buttons? If it is merely the shape of the button that is being brought into play, or its virtual shape, this initially seems less interesting. Perhaps there is something telling about the values we have come to attach to the concept of button-ness.

Since it is poets who make it their business to be aware how metaphors work, and where they spring from, it may be useful to look at how they employ the idea of buttons and buttoning. One of the things poets do is to

6. Lava bee, mid-nineteenth century.

bring to the surface of our awareness what has become forgotten through too frequent usage. From this perspective, attempting to bear down on these button-inspired metaphors may help reveal some of the hidden meaning within our everyday usage. For example, to ask someone to button their lip, more than just asking them to be quiet, suggests they make a specific effort, parallel to pushing a button through a buttonhole, pressing one lip firmly over the other. One could further argue there might be something brutal about conjuring up such an image, imagining the button as having been sewn through the sensitive flesh of the mouth, and in turn the buttonhole becoming an open, sucking wound. To button your lip then becomes something disturbing and suggests a withheld, perhaps subconscious, aggression on the part of the speaker. The currently widely used expression of pressing or pushing my button, to describe being pleased by some act or attitude, and which may initiate or arouse a response, suggests something fairly gentle, if insistent. It has a very different connotation from the image of, say, 'ringing my bell', and yet because of the sensual images it draws on, if one imagines a single finger tip pressing on a button, it remains less passive than a more ethereal expression such as 'floating my boat'. 'Pushing the button' can have a negative connotation, as if a button-switch is being repeatedly, irritatingly, impressed:

> You couldn't push my buttons if you tried. In fact, I have no buttons. Please think of me as buttonless, all smooth like GI Joe's nether-regions.

> (Dr Cox attempting to threaten in ABC TV's *Scrubs*, 2001)

However, in everyday metaphorical usage, it is common for the actual graphic image – of the button that joins together two pieces of cloth, say – to fade from view. Most common metaphors tend to disappear: we become so used to them that they no longer make us think of the vehicle that is being used in its original non-metaphorical sense, so deeply have they become part of our everyday language. If I say of someone that they are 'on the button', I may not necessarily bring to mind, or want to bring to mind, the comparison being made. It would be appallingly tedious if one were to recall each and every metaphorical connection and get in the way of present-time usage.

Yet there sometimes needs to remain some distance between the object being referred to and an ordinary button, and often this distance can create a meaningful friction. For example, when Lear, on hearing that the Fool is dead, asks Kent to 'undo this button' (*King Lear*, act V, scene 3), it is in one sense a literal request (he is distressed and thus overheated, wanting to be rid of his coat) but it is also an appeal for emotional release, presaging his own madness. In comparison, in *Hamlet*, when Guildenstern claims, 'On Fortune's cap we are not the very button' (act I, scene 2), the use of the metaphor is initially more straightforward. We understand that he and Rosencrantz are not content, as in not being like the button at the centre of its cap, but the meaning is then expanded by Hamlet so that the button comes to stand for the head or intellect, in opposition to Fortune's feet, thus allowing for the more complex trope. What lurks between buttoned cap and feet becomes Fortune's 'privates', and thus Hamlet can deliver his punch line: 'In the secret parts of Fortune? Oh most true: she is a strumpet...' The idea of Fortune being mercenary was not original, and in making such hackneyed wordplay, with a stock button image, the lack of genuine humour in Hamlet's mood is revealed.

One could put forward yet more button-based language, and I shall be looking in more detail at some of its specific applications, but the important point here is that, increasingly, and particularly from the mid-eighteenth century on, the button has encroached on our culture not only through its role in clothes and fashion but also as an idea of buttoning and unbuttoning, of being buttoned or not, and that this continues to affect us all – so much so that we can hardly speak, or think, without invoking the idea of the button.

Yet how does this backdrop, this referencing back and forth between actual button and its imagery, influence the collector and what draws the collector to collect?

CHAPTER TWO

Why We Collect

With crayons the child draws a rigid house and
a winding pathway. Then the child puts in a man
with buttons like tears...

(Elizabeth Bishop, *Sestina*, 1956)

In this poem a grandmother tries to be cheerful with her grandchild, and the absent mother seems to lie between them, unmentioned (Ryan, 2007, p. 103). The grandmother is reading jokes from an almanac as she drinks tea from a cup, 'full of dark brown tears'. Almanacs are meant to foretell the future, based on the patterns of the past, events, tides, the phases of the moon, and here the 'little moons' of buttons, when the moon has long symbolized change and unreliability, 'fall down like tears...into the flower bed' that the child is drawing.

Buttons are evoking a sad past event that we, the reader, are not given the details of, and that we come to feel both child and older woman are trying to avoid.

Buttons are able to represent this pull of a lost past and one may find it difficult to disregard. The business of collecting tends to play upon the mixed pleasure and pain that nostalgia brings. To choose to collect buttons suggests a nature drawn to this interface between the hard truths of our mortality and a more sentimental belief that we can somehow hang on to comforting aspects of what is irrevocably lost. As a child I liked the button tin, but I was only dimly aware of its significance. Although there are examples of young collectors, it seems nonetheless generally true that most have lived long enough to begin to taste the threat of their own mortality. The antiques expert Adrian Grater took up button collecting on his daughter's behalf. Buttons are given to her for birthdays and Christmas, yet he remains the caretaker, and the collection is guided by his taste and knowledge.

In recent decades the market for vintage clothing and accessories has flourished. The designer Cath Kidston sells her shabby-chic look, including new but worn-looking floral button tins. In Britain, in the retail market, the clothing company Toast promotes its nostalgic look with typical hand-knitted style cardigans, and Boden is known for its signature buttons, often childlike, brightly coloured and oversized. In a more insidious take, the Claudette label, for example, recycles old textiles, incorporating old buttons, sometimes used to conceal holes in patchworked cashmere pieces. There is an abundance of craftwork involving buttons. We are in an age of nostalgia. In one sense the practical business of collating and the sheer magnitude of the task once one begins to look into the history of each button distracts the collector from other concerns, and its difficulties and appeal provide a sentimental barricading against the unknown future. Moreover, in the case of the button, we are collecting something essentially human, made for a human purpose directly associated with our frail, temporal bodies, and at its height button collecting represents Culture as opposed to random, impervious Nature.

What draws people to take up collecting? It is said that collectors collect to collect. Benjamin Button's father's button factory encourages him to see familiarity with buttons as a significant character trait:

> Some people were born to sit by a river. Some people get struck by lightning. Some people have an ear for music. Some swim. Some know buttons…
>
> (*The Curious Case of Benjamin Button*, 2008)

Not everyone collects, of course. Some fear too many possessions, and the idea of replicating similar objects can seem oppressive, like a cat forced to live at close quarters with litter after litter of her progeny, in claustrophobic proximity to what should naturally be long gone. Yet even among non-collectors, many are fascinated by collections, and impressed by the efforts of those who have laboured to acquire them. Knowledge relies in part on the comparing and sifting of masses of examples of similar objects, and without the collectors' work this would be impossible, particularly in relation to artefacts not obviously recognized as of interest at the time. If only, if only I had not gone and downsized, had not life-laundried my Great-Aunt Monica's collection of stuffed dodos…

The collector deliberately gathers together an accumulation of objects. People's choice of what they collect often appears to reveal something about their inner character. For

7. *Passementerie,* embroidered and mother-of-pearl buttons, early nineteenth century.

example, Jackie Kennedy Onassis collecting rare French enamel buttons may have been a reaction to an earlier prohibition regarding the wearing of her favoured French couturiers, but equally it might just mean she was interested in the eighteenth century and loved buttons. Similarly, in collecting French army uniform buttons, Charles de Gaulle may not have been exposing an unconscious desire to convince all of his patriotism. If you ask button collectors why they might not prefer to collect some other fandangle, then they may offer up fascinating anecdotes to explain how their interest began, but it is much more difficult to get to the root of their drive to collect. They can seem defensive, and one needs to tread carefully, not to seem part of an uncomprehending opposition. Any form of collecting can be viewed by those who do not collect as strangely single-minded, and sometimes to demand an amount of attention disproportionate to the objects accrued. The more obviously financially valuable a collection, the better it is respected by those who are otherwise ignorant.

Nevertheless, one suspects it is the act of collecting and not the things in themselves that often drive people to find more objects. People bargain and sell to have room to collect more. People sell a collection of beer mats in order to begin to collect coins, or sell their coins for an idea they have of a grand assemblage of buttons. They may say, 'I cannot decide what to collect next.' Something seems missing in their lives until a new enthusiasm is embraced. There also exist those who are drawn to collect all and everything, driven by a desire to accumulate whatever happens to become accessible to them, whatever answers their taste and feeds their need.

At my local branch meeting of the British Button Society I was met with a groan of recognition when I mentioned that this book had been sparked off by affection for an inherited box of buttons. The members clearly knew each other well and fondly, and there was an atmosphere of serious attention as each showed the examples they had brought along. Several times I was gently warned how vast was the subject and near impossible to contain within a book. It was clear to me that this sense of expansive knowledge required to understand buttons thrilled them.

Each meeting has a form of 'show and tell' of a different letter of the alphabet and subject: ours was T and Transport. I tried to take photographs in the half-light, realizing that as I fussed and squinted, I was missing some new bit of information. I was also holding up the circulation of the evidence. I saw a tortoiseshell toucan, four inches long, with shiny beak and its head feathers formed from the knobby protuberances of the untreated shell, which led to a discussion of Guinness promotional buttons. I was shown enamel toucans and told of a trompe l'oeil picture button, under glass and framed in brass, of a toucan beside a foaming glass of Guinness, probably once worn on the waistcoat of a publican; I saw modern ceramic buttons based on Picasso drawings (one of which had *t*oes); there were buttons from the days of bicycle fever, railway buttons, tube buttons, liveries with horses' heads, a skier; a wooden turbot had been offered at the last meeting as a salmon when S was the dish of the day, resulting in much ribaldry; a recent Tutankhamen exhibition was discussed; the Pearly Kings and Queens service at St Martin in the Fields, I learnt, was held on the first Sunday in October; the town of Faversham was praised for its new button shop. One member was planning to interest the backers of Jenson Button with a memorial button and sought more ideas for the design. My neighbour, Suzanne Barr, explained that another name for the corozo nut was tagua, and handed me something like a heavy, slightly uneven goose egg, so hard that she had not been able to stab it with a red hot needle (I was anxious not to miss a photograph button of a Cheshire Cat at the time, but I gather the needle reveals whether it retains a consistency suitable for intricate carving). She suggested I read about the Duchess of Devonshire who had encountered a lord wearing obscene buttons on his waistcoat and told me about prostitutes' 'knob' buttons (see Chapter 8). The group recommended I consult Jane Perry's *Peasant Silver* when I was puzzled by something that looked less like a button and rather more like the droplet handles on a sideboard. It was, in sum, two hours of intense sharing of information, and I was impressed and loathe to explain that I was not really a collector at all, but just trying to gasp what it was that drove them.

One of the pleasures many claim in collecting is the oblique way in which historical and cultural knowledge is gradually accrued. This may be so, and is often so in the case of the button, but the variety of ways in which collectors have come to the task suggest that the motivation is more complex and deep-rooted than merely a desire for an intelligent pastime. There is more often a serious emotional investment in collections that are, to the outsider, trivial or random. Should the collector move on to a new subject of collecting, then the strength of emotion moves with them to the new area, leaving the previously revered items bled of personal value.

Roger Cardinal, in his article 'Collecting and Collage Making: The Case of Kurt Schwitters', uses the example of the German Dada artist to dissect the stages a collector moves through. He makes the important point that collection and collector can be inseparable, so that the sense collectors have of refining their choices and developing a better idea of what does and does not belong may be near impossible for another to fully comprehend.

What is the process button collectors go through in building up a collection? What fuels their categories and creates a sense of order? Some collectors are bent on finding out as much as they can about the particulars of the buttons' historical journey before they came into their possession, whereas others may want to see them merely in their correct historical context. They seem immune to the romance of the journey.

Cardinal describes the state of mind the collector hopes his activity will bring about as being 'to invent a space of privileged equilibrium' (p. 70), so our button collector seeks a private state of mind, where they will feel freed from everyday troubles. The trouble is that even so relatively gentle an activity as button collecting can provide its own pressures, in the difficulties of acquisition, seeking bargains, deftly trouncing a rival, or being oneself piped to the post of the perfectly appropriate find. Even the small difficulties inherent in any serious-minded collecting endeavour can provide its own tensions. Attempting to adapt Cardinal's stages to buttons in particular:

1. Collectors must prospect for finds.
2. They need to purchase or somehow acquire new buttons.
3. Once the buttons have been obtained, they are taken to a private space and ritually unpacked by the new owner.
4. Sifting through a tin, collectors identify which buttons are relevant.

5. They disregard or reject what seems irrelevant. Sometimes a collector may desire only singles, and sell on the rest of an acquired set.

6. Examining new finds, cleaning, deciding on their composition, they 'fondle and polish'.

7. The additions to the collection are arranged, labelled and numbered and the date of each acquisition duly noted.

Even if a collector rejects some aspect of this method, I suspect they will recognize a sense of ordered ritual in the pleasure they find in collecting. Some collectors have presentation files, beautifully created; others prefer to keep their buttons in self-seal bags or CD cases; some keep their finds' original wrapping, their newspaper, paper bags, bubble wrap and matchboxes, in part perhaps to retain something of their first unwrapping. Adding to the sense of ceremony are the specialist words that are applied, like the gardener with the correct Latin names or the computer buff with all the newest jargon. This new vocabulary reinforces the collectors' sense of their privileged, specialized knowledge: *églomisé*, *kagagami-buta*, *strass* and *pietra dura* seem exotic and even the button-specific application of foil, realistic, habitat, goofy – all contribute to a sense of a privileged world apart.

Because the button has been used at all levels and across many societies, collecting can be an inroad into many subjects, such as manufacturing techniques; it can lead to scientific investigation to decipher their make-up, encourage travel to investigate new markets, involve the thrill of bargaining amd meeting other collectors. The business of searching for buttons connects in an organic way with grander themes that might otherwise have

8. Grayson Perry, *Artist's Robe*, 2004.

seemed off-putting or too portentous. Anne Blight, a long-term member of the British Button Society, related how her initial curiosity led her to read about subjects that she would have been unlikely otherwise to have tackled. She was, for example, particularly taken with buttons that she later discovered to be designed by the Italian artist Piero Fornasetti. This brought her into contact with the surrealist movement and also with the idea that an artist's work could be dominated by a recurring image, in Fornasetti's case that of the soprano Lina Cavalieri, whose lovely iconic face still adorns so many textiles, wallpapers, plates and T-shirts. In like manner the pottery buttons of Dame Lucie Rie (Chapter 9) encouraged Blight to look at the artist's other works and further to consider the role of craft and manufacture in her button hobby. She feels that falling into button collecting has, in retrospect, given her 'a whole new life'. I would like to suggest that in fact collecting is a way of confirming a sense of self that her pastime has made possible.

The huge variety of buttons available must be part of the attraction: Dorset worked buttons, made from thread and scraps of knitting wool, worn linen underwear buttons, cheap mass-produced plastics at one extreme, and high-end studio ceramics, cut steel, precious jewel-encrusted, *passe-menterie*, worked silver and gold at the other, all encompass the collector's vision. Some collectors limit themselves to particular areas or types of button – many, more often men, specialize in military buttons, livery, political, maritime and uniforms in general. As I examine the Button Society membership directory, the variety of specializations is great, and variously defined. People say they are interested squarely in Art Nouveau, the eighteenth century or British Colonial, in specific materials only such as

9. Rare Austro-Hungarian eighteenth-century marvels in silver, enamelled, and set with rubies and diamonds.

black glass or enamel, or they define manufacturers, such as Bimini or Satsuma.

Other categories of interest include dress, museum, modern, fashion, insurance, royal, police, livery, early decorative, paste, tinies, shell, backmarks, whistles, vegetable ivory, button brooches, archery, railway, silver – tourist and peasant, British Transport, cut steel, clocks, Hammond Turner, heads, mother-of-pearl, wooden, floral, Austrian, Sherwood Foresters, cats, pictures, hunt, Arts and Crafts, tramway, canal, omnibus, volunteers, military pipers, Art Deco, celluloid, Fire Brigade, yacht, Victorian, Cornish, Jennens, yeomanry, Golden Age, mental health, orphanage, workhouse, Indian Army volunteers, dogs, yak bone buttons from Nepal and asylums.

This is not a complete list, and though it may seem to lead nowhere, as in Gertrude Stein's inventories in her poetic prose work *Tender Buttons*, it has been selected and arranged. In this sense it has some measure of classification. I was led by the sound of some, the idea I had of others and perhaps omitted collections that I dare say are of great interest but that did not happen to catch my attention. Those members who seem led more freely by their own sense of aesthetic preference, or perhaps have yet to decide on their specialization, say they collect 'all' or 'any', but they surely mean all or any that they happen to like. The collector can be supremely, sometimes idiosyncratically, subjective and yet attend with seriousness to their chosen field, with wider reading, checking their tentative findings against the scholarship of others – in fact drawing on aspects of scientifically objective and intellectually rigorous enquiry.

It is difficult to acquire pre-nineteenth century examples, for they are expensive and hard to come by. But their diversity helps to explain how modern buttons are so

various, and, more than this, they are the key to why buttons have gained the position they hold in our culture.
Martyn Frith of the London shop The Button Queen
pointed out that British cloth historically has long been
particularly highly valued. Our wool cloth is renowned
for being of fine quality, especially the tweeds and melton
cloth, georgettes and finer varunas, woollen damasks and
failles – fabric, it is said, that one might draw through a
ring to prove its worth. This reputation means that traditionally there has been less interest in trimmings and fin-
ishings than in continental Europe, where more emphasis
has fallen on linings, bindings and buttons to enrich a garment. British buttons tended to be thus more understated,
allowing the quality of the fabric to speak for itself. Plain
bone buttons were made to last as long as their accompa-
nying worsted overcoat, and simple but strong, well-made
plastic buttons were not made to star, but to play a supporting role on a garment.

These days it is common to see top high street stores
using relatively poor quality buttons. The late Jean Muir
was noted for the taste and refinement of her buttons, one
amongst many examples being the sunflower yellow coat,
huge buckle and button in deep scarlet Perspex – a garment to yearn for (Stemp, 2006). I suspect she might raise
an elegant brow at those now sold on designs selling in
her name, so inferior are they in relation to the quality of
fabric and design. Sometimes a designer will allow shoddy
buttons that nonetheless advertise their trademark name.
This degradation conforms to the bottom line economics of
capitalism, where margins are continually being cut. Italian
and French designer buttons seem to have maintained their
quality better than those in the UK; one might also suggest
that in the UK this tendency stems from the ongoing effects

of Benthamite utilitarianism, a button still fulfilling its function well enough, even if it has become cheaper and uglier.

In order to gauge the intrinsic value of a button, as
against what might be the market value at any one time,
the skill of the craft involved must be set against the value
of the materials. The small size of buttons calls on the craftsperson being able to work in small scale, which requires
great dexterity. The artist who might wish to paint a miniature scene on a button has to learn how to produce an
assured line, but when such a line is greatly reduced in
scale, the same assurance is much more difficult to achieve,
with an eyelash brush held in a hand still of human scale.
If, for example, a miniature painting by Levina Teerlinc or
Nicholas Hilliard in the sixteenth century is valued in part
for being in wondrous miniature, then a button, derived
from such artists and sometimes still further reduced in
scale, must take on some of that wonder. Fragonard, pupil
of both Chardin and Boucher, was adept at painting buttons in the manner of Watteau, depicting idyllic yet fleeting
frivolity, in verdant scenes of amorous couples, gorgeously
silk-arrayed young women and playful cherubs. Similarly
the fashion for the scaling down of classical images or
Renaissance portraits to illustrate buttons draws on the
concept of *multum in parvo*, as in William Blake's 'Auguries
of Innocence' (1803):

> To see a world in a grain of sand
> And a Heaven in a wild flower
> Hold Infinity in the palm of your hand...

There is something about the fact that the button is
man-made that gives it value. We know from science that
the world of nature is potentially infinitely divisible, and

that, at least for most of us, it is beyond our understanding. We hear of the numerous patterns of a snowflake, of the minutiae of DNA profiles, the ever-diminishing propensities of a black hole, of the potential of a mathematical theory of division like Zeno's paradox, where every journey is divisible by half ad infinitum, and so our ultimate arrival remains forever beyond our reach.

Buttons mirror some of this sense of marvellous detail but in a way that can be taken on board. The button can be a miracle of artisan skill and aesthetics, where sometimes skill can override the subject matter. It is a graspable entity, offering something of infinity that can be held in the palm of your hand and seen by natural eyesight. A friend reckons her love of small objects is akin to feeling that she is herself safely, cosily confined. Perhaps such contemplation makes us feel childlike again, reminding us of a time when we were able to focus more intently, when once we felt small ourselves, in a land of towering adults who did not notice that detailed wonder. With this parallel in mind, Susan Stewart notes (1993, p. 57) that the first dolls were initially adult playthings. Catherine de' Medici, for example, had eight fashion dolls, and their miniature up-to-the-minute clothes, with minute diamond and gilded buttons, allowed her to move between the interior world of her imagination and her otherwise full-scale reality.

Stewart suggests that it is often only the abstract idea of miniature worlds that are really made available to us. We delight perhaps in the watercolour illustrations of Beatrix Potter, partly because we love to see the miniature domestic worlds of her small animal protagonists. Yet the buttons on Peter Rabbit's blue jacket are in reality no smaller drawn than the buttons of Jack and the Beanstalk's giant, in a similar-sized illustration. We can only 'see' that the stitches the mice make for the buttonholes, in *The Tailor of Gloucester*, are miniscule, because we have been told they are made by mice. There is nothing in the drawings that can show this, yet we experience them as exceptionally small in our imagination's eye. The miniature only exists in relation to ourselves: it relies on our sense of relative comparison.

The metal detector has brought many people unwittingly to button collecting. What could be a better example of a method that has all the fun of a fairground game and yet holds the promise of hidden treasure creating a taste for playing detective, in order to begin to understand what they find? Many a hoard of ancient buttons has turned up in garden or field. A particularly rich source of treasure is the 'black jelly of the Thames' (Bainbridge), once the city of London's main highway. It is probable that for as long as people have travelled its waters, poorer folk have eked out a living sifting through the mudflats at low tide for anything of value, dropped or washed into the river from the drains. An atmosphere of disreputable, sinister goings-on at the beginning of Charles Dickens's *Our Mutual Friend* (1865) has Lizzie and her father on its filthy waters, in the middle of the night in a tiny rowing boat, the girl unwilling to get near whatever it is that they are towing to shore. Dickens heightens the tension by never specifying exactly what it is her father, the 'hawk', has discovered, though we come to realize it is a corpse. He sees himself as in a different moral category from those who take from living men, for why should the river keep hold of valuable buttons when the dead have no use for them?

Cutpurses might get rid of their victims by throwing them into the water, so that these corpses and those of suicides and drowned sailors could then be harvested for any remaining clothes, including buttons, of course. This was a despised job, mainly left to children and widowed women, bringing the risk of sewage-borne disease, being swept away by tides or marooned in a sucking mud bed. It was also illegal, and practitioners came to be known as mudlarks, a slang term for pigs.

Nowadays mudlarks are respected members of a small society alone licensed to trawl the Thames mud for treasure. Recently, Tony Pilson, who has been mudlarking for 30 years, donated a collection of over 2,500 buttons and cufflinks, dating back to medieval times, to the Museum of London. 'It's the luck of the draw,' he remarked, 'the uncertainty of what you might find that makes it so appealing.' He is pictured in the press gazing up into the camera, like a genial pirate with his booty, amid trays filled with row upon row of buttons. It is noteworthy that his role has been depicted as something of an explorer, and I suspect this is related not only to our relative affluence today and to the rarity of these finds, but also to our desire for the romance of swashbuckling adventure.

The several articles about this enterprise stress a possible financial value as much as the buttons' historical merit. One claimed that many of the buttons found were worth in their day a great sum, another that they might now be valued at over five times that amount, and yet another that the entire haul might raise a king's ransom. Be that as it may, Pilson's donation of this collection shows not only his generosity but also points to the desire a serious collector has to properly display his finds, and to have those finds honoured. What could be more appropriate in this respect than having a museum fully record, research and catalogue his discoveries? With evident zeal he wants to encourage other metal detectors to share their finds, adding that 'the more we find, the less and less there is left to discover'.

I would argue that this sense of increasing rarity adds to collectors' non-commercial, spiritual sense of value. What is hard to come by becomes for many the source of sentimental attachment and of nostalgic power. As we fear our own mortality, so we want to protect what should be capable of survival, as if to do so shores us up against the shifting tide.

Many hobbyists still run up against the prejudice that they are akin to collectors of beer mats, wasting their time with things of no value or significant provenance. Even if this were true – regarding buttons or indeed beer mats – I think the non-collector misconstrues the instinct that drives people to collect. Collecting is a fundamental drive, as natural to some as to the squirrel or magpie, but such collections are fuelled by intellect. Those who do not collect rely on the collector, so that one can know that this vast panoply of diverse detailed knowledge is potentially available.

There are buttons that were never intended to last. Their essentially ephemeral nature can nonetheless be valued highly by the collector, their tender substance forming a parallel with our own lives, like a cardboard button and string fastening, laminated paper-thin craftwork buttons, the button snaps on nappies or the throwaway fibre buttons on disposable clothing of the 1960s, paper clothing glories in its fragility. Because of the current interest in the threatened environment, artists have brought this quality into focus with deliberately impermanent clothing. Later in this book I want to take a look at the way artists have utilized more conventional buttons to implicitly relate to our consumer culture, however Charlotte Stockdale chose

10. British Button Society AGM, 2009.

to make paper clothing with a group of couturiers and designers (*British Vogue*, April 2007). Using buttons that at times look like the filigree of shells, but are in fact rolled and pleated paper, she describes their appeal as being that they are easily suited to a wide range of styling techniques. There is pride in their exotic provenance, for she mentions 'rare bamboo-leaf sheaves from as far afield as Tokyu Hands', a cult department store in Tokyo. Other varieties of paper are hunted down in Paris or ordered from specialist bookbinders, but some of the decisions she makes stem from a sense of what seems relevant to the garment in hand, and not merely to being able to fulfil their function.

As Stockdale and her workshop developed their ideas, more of the inherent qualities of paper were brought into play. Cardboard was used when strength, tissue when transparency was required, but, more abstractly, the associations we have with different sorts of paper were utilized. Thus a corset is made from old Vogue patterns, a raincoat of Ordnance Survey maps, recalling the paper follies Cecil Beaton used as sets for his beautifully manicured photo shoots, where the exquisite panache of the models contrasts with the ephemeral and low-value associations attached to paper.

Buttons have often been made from surplus materials, not only fabric remnants but, say, plastic buttons manufactured from clippings from aeroplane windscreens. Epstein and Safro mention the use of leftover acrylic from bomber gun-turrets in the Second World War being transformed into pretty floral buttons. Such an association can delight the collector but may contribute to the comic or trivial associations we have with buttons, or to their being seen as intrinsically of very little significance, made from materials originally resourced for something of greater importance.

The dedicated collector is of enormous importance to our cultures across the world, without which the great museum collections would not exist and our ability to garner knowledge from the past would be limited. There would be the remains of memories handed down, the evidence of the written word and in modern history of film and recorded sound. Yet where would be the ephemera that serve our imagination, the concrete artefacts, be they even so small as the button? And so, what is the historical background to this button collecting habit? When did buttons become prevalent enough and of sufficient diversity for the collections to begin?

Collections to visit:

Bolton Museum
The British Museum, London
Brixham Heritage Museum, Devon
City of Birmingham Museum and Art Gallery
Cooper-Hewitt Museum of Design, New York
Den Gamle By, Arhus, Denmark
Edinburgh Castle: houses the National War Museum of
    Scotland
Essex Institute Salem, Massachusetts
The Fashion Museum, Bath
The Foundling Museum, London
Historisch Kostuum Museum, Utrecht, Netherlands
Jablone, Museum of Glass and Jewellery, Czech
    Republic: lacy glass
The Keep Homestead Museum, Monson, Massachusetts
Kensington Palace: eighteenth century onwards, Royal
    Ceremonial Dress Collection, London
Kirkaldy Museum, Fifeshire
Ludenschied, Märkischer Kreis, Germany

Manchester City Galleries, Platt Hall (by appointment only)

Metropolitan Museum of Art, New York: Hanna Sicher Kohn Collection

Musée de la Mode, Paris

Musée de la Mosaïque et des Émaux, Briare, France

Museum of Costume, Bath

Museum of the Confederacy, Richmond, Virginia

The National Army Museum, London

The National Maritime Museum, Greenwich, London

Pennsylvania House Museum, Springfield

Strong Museum, Rochester, New York: Margaret Strong Collection

Tokyo Button Museum, Japan

Vermont Virtual Civil War Museum

Victoria and Albert Museum, London

Waddesdon Manor, Buckinghamshire: de Rothschild Collection

Waldes Museum, Prague, Czech Republic

CHAPTER THREE

The Enlightenment Button

Man's earthly interests are all hooked and buttoned
together, and held up by clothes

(Thomas Carlyle, *Sartor Resartus*, 1833–4,
bk. 1, vol. 8)

The golden age of the button, in Europe of the
eighteenth century, coincides with new ideas that
changed the make-up of the Western world. How
much of this is a coincidence and how did buttons
benefit from or even contribute to this transformation?

Its beginnings are presaged in the court dress of the
sixteenth and seventeenth centuries. The royal courts of
Europe were a fulcrum for the display of power between
nations, and dress was an obvious way of demonstrating this
battle for pre-eminence. This may not have been fashion as
we have come to conceive of it, but there were fine clothes
and fine buttons upon them. Monarchs and their courtiers
vied with other nations for the most gorgeous apparel. Even
the Dutch court, which from the mid-sixteenth century

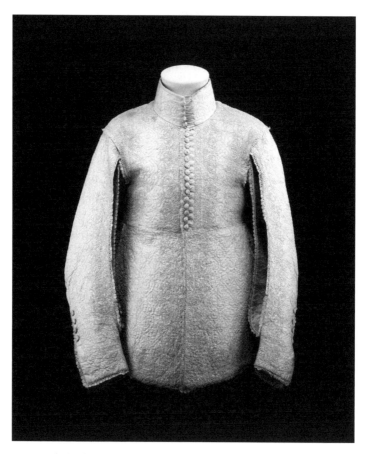

11. English doublet, glazed linen with *passementerie* buttons: linen thread hand-plaited over a wooden core, 1635–40.

was beginning to wear subdued clothing in line with non-conformist religious precepts, wore discreetly sumptuous garb that still managed to impose its value on the onlooker. Similarly for the Catholic Spanish court, the zealotry of the Counter-Reformation and the Inquisition fostered a fashion for lavish black clothing that glittered with jewelled and facetted buttons, sombre yet impressive.

In the thirteenth and fourteenth centuries there was a mania for excessive embellishment, sometimes leaving hardly any portion of a garment free of decorative or functioning buttons. King Francis I of France ordered 13,400 gold buttons for a black velvet suit for his state meeting with Henry VII of England. The two kings vied with each other in their lavish buttoning. Like two stags drawn, there needed to be a parity of display, antler to antler. One has only to study the portraits of the time to marvel at the gorgeously studded satins and brocades. They relied on an elaborate display of impractical and hard come by materials, in the main gold, silver, precious jewels and gemstones got with great difficulty and expense.

Elizabeth I's gowns were studded with ornate, jewelled buttons in all manner of forms. *Elizabeth R* cites contemporary accounts of 'two buttons of gold like tortoises' (Strong and Trevelyan Oman, 2007, p. 25) in relation to them having been lost, which suggests they must have been of considerable value for such a fact to be recorded, and a dress with 'fourteen buttons embroidered like butterflies, with flower pearles and one emerode in a pece, lined with cloth of sylver, prented'. Precious metals were set with diamonds and gemstones, and handmade covered buttons embroidered with her coat of arms and other royal insignia. Around 1625, the First Duke of Buckingham reputedly had a suit and cloak made entirely

covered in diamond buttons (although it is said they may
have been of cheaper rock crystal) and King Louis XIV of
France spent fortunes on buttons, bankrupting his coffers.
Epstein mentions how Louis gave Mlle d'Abigne a bridal
gift of 16 sleeve buttons, valued at 12,000 francs. When
monarchs did not meet, their portraits might be exchanged,
and the artists' job was to demonstrate their paymasters'
status and wealth with lavish depictions, which more often
than not included a glittering array of buttons.

The exquisite passementerie button, a woven and
embroidered button rich with ornamentation, originating
from France in the late thirteenth century and becoming
popular again in the sixteenth century, required many
hours of meticulous, skilled workmanship. Victor Houart
mentions several types of French passementerie: *à poives*,
glands, *vases*, *olives*, *piqués* and *jaserons*. Some were embellished with jet, some steel, sequins, pearls, gold, silver
and mother-of-pearl and later, in the nineteenth century,
beaded passementerie was produced. The wedding suit
of James II (1673) can be found at the V&A, with silver embroidered passementerie buttons. Although the
waistcoat is now missing, which would have had another
row of such buttons probably slightly smaller in size,
the jacket and trousers, all in the same embroidered pale
wool, are said to represent the beginnings of the modern
three-piece suit.

Precious stones and metals had to be obtained for the
jewellers to provide sufficiently dazzling bibelots to satisfy the button appetite. Gold and silver woven into rich
wool and silk fabrics were used, metallic thread worked
into their structure. Usually such buttons were stuffed
and sometimes further felted, in order to harden and
strengthen them. Some were built over a wooden core,

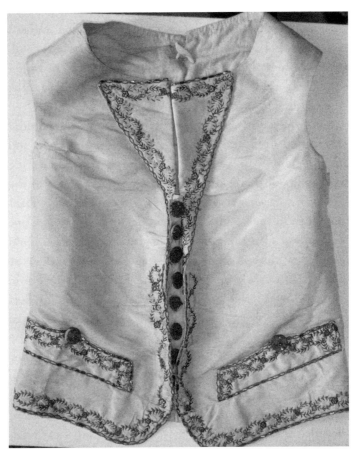

12. Child's waistcoat, early eighteenth century, silk embroidery on silk cloth with faceted steel buttons.

a fretwork of thread covering the base in various patterns of ladders, pinwheels and spirals, usually over a basic more simply covered layer. This structure could then be embroidered to create further texture and pattern and could then be ornamented with jewels. As with other skilled trades – silk and wool merchants, jewellers, tailors, printers, silversmiths and goldsmiths – these button makers, or rather their overseers, became wealthy and began to emulate the styles of their patrons.

As the eighteenth century wore on, the button established itself as a more available sign of wealth and status. The newly wealthy had economic means and the beginnings of political power, largely independent of the monarchy. Clothes had denoted rank alone, but now fashion began to emerge in all its metamorphoses. Though one is speaking of a thin slice of society, anyone who could afford new clothes might have them. The new science, the idea of nature as a central, guiding force and a belief in man's value as based on individual capacities and intellect rather than birthright – all are mirrored in the journey of the button.

Thorstein Veblen describes this process of a flourishing new class, the new money, for whom possession of property became the basis of self-esteem and of feeling better or worse than one's fellows. Moreover, though these makers and merchants gained their position through their labours initially, it soon became important for them to abstain from that work. Anything that smacked of 'menial offices' might lower their standing. Clothes were a means of distinguishing them from those involved in vulgar, sweaty labour. Veblen called their ability to consume such luxuries 'conspicuous consumption'. So far, women in this drama of shifting power are

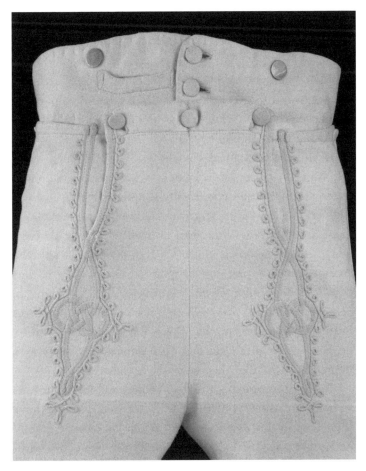

13. Pantaloons, early trousers, worn tight – sometimes known as 'tights'. This pair is of machine-knitted cotton with selfcovered buttons. Although they were fashionable during 1810–20s, aping the glamour of the military, these may well have been actual uniform, as the Austrian knot pattern was a popular motif of the light cavalry.

still waiting in the wings, playing no significant economic role. They may have formed part of the sometimes skilled labour force, but they could not be members of a guild or hold capital in their names. They had no more legitimacy than a child.

Men's clothes were again becoming more fitted and jackets began to extend to mid-calf, so that a fashionable outfit would have to involve greater numbers of buttons, down the centre opening, as well as those along pocket flaps, sleeves, back pleat, the new waistcoat, breeches and yet more on boots and gloves. As the century gathered pace, clothing became gradually simpler in style. Quentin Bell (1976) describes more distinctions being drawn in dress for different functions, as well as a new division being made between uniform and civilian wear. The change towards greater simplicity meant that it was possible for a man of comparatively modest means to achieve unimpeachable style, but it also called for greater button production, in that there were now many more people who required buttons, even if for men it became no longer requisite that they be of the highest value.

It was becoming possible for women of moderate means to begin to collect, but those of great wealth might have their pick of fine early buttons. When Baroness Edmond de Rothschild (1853–1935) decided to collect eighteenth-century buttons, she could not have known how useful they would prove to highlight both the momentum of the Enlightenment and its slicker aftermath. She is said to have been driven by a love of dressing up and regularly wore her buttons and old lace, for she had previously been a collector of lace, fans and seals before coming to buttons. She collected over 600 individual buttons, forming 60 sets in all manner of materials and crafts.

Beginning to collect at a time when buttons had again become fashionable for women, the items in her collection came from a time when they were intended almost exclusively for men. Women might have fine buttons on their masculine-tailored riding jackets, or, towards the end of the century, some wore short-waisted jackets, *à la Suzanne*, named after Susanna in Beaumarchais's comedy *The Marriage of Figaro* (1784). However, in the main, the Baroness, in sporting her finds, was inadvertently subverting their intended gender.

Diana Scarisbrook describes the eighteenth-century button as being 'not so much a practical fastening as an ornament which emphasized the cut of the coat, reflected light and expressed *joie de vivre*'. But of course its fastening properties did allow it to show off a man's figure. The most aberrant example of this male display can be seen in the Macaronis, and described by Amanda Foreman as wearing 'large buttons and extravagant nosegays (which) were essential' (*Georgiana, Duchess of Devonshire*, 1999). The song 'Yankee Doodle' draws on a shared knowledge of such fops to mock the gauche Yankee, who thinks he can become fashionable with little sartorial effort:

> Yankee Doodle went to town
> A riding on a pony,
> He stuck a feather in his cap
> And called it macaroni!

Young men, influenced by the fashions they had witnessed on the Grand Tour, adopted tightly buttoned jackets which had the effect of absurdly lengthening the trunk, and their buttons were often enormous, worn

14. Nellie Collier collage, *That Damned Elusive Pimpernel*, 2009. Clockwise from top right: Macaronis, 1940s English gentleman, James Bond, the Prince Regent, Cecil Beaton, eighteenth-century fop and Jumping Jack Flash. Centre: Leslie Howard in the film of *The Scarlet Pimpernel* (1934) with the elegant cuffs of President Obama.

with outsized, powdered, perfumed and bouffant wigs. This was often topped off with miniscule tilting hats, so high up that they could only be removed with the tip of a sword. This trend for the pouter-pigeon silhouette and trousers that fitted like peach skin reminds one of characters such as Sir Percy Blakeney in Emmuska Orczy's *The Scarlet Pimpernel*, who gives the impression he thinks of nothing but his appearance, but in fact regularly risks life and limb to rescue aristocrats from the guillotine. The theme of the fey popinjay, who is in reality a man of courage and intellect, becomes a popular one in literature. This sense that such effeminacy of style might be a pose is a prelude to the idea of the thinking dandy of the nineteenth century. However, the periwigged fop was nonetheless a last flowering of colourful male excess, practically until the 'glorious plumage' of the 1960s: the wild party before the dismal dark uniformity that has hardly altered since.

Outsize buttons can infantilize, for like the miniature characters in Mary Norton's *The Borrowers*, or on the front of a circus clown's all-in-one, the wearer is dwarfed in proportion, the body made to seem consequently fragile or foolish, hardly up to bearing their weight. Outsized buttons are a recurring theme in women's couture, and in 2006 there was a trend on the catwalks for oversized buttons on men's overcoats and jackets, but they were understated in colour and the fashion never reached the high street – prompting the suggestion that such buttons are not in keeping with contemporary ideas of masculinity. The artist Kiki van Eijk, marketed her white and pearl finished stoneware plates, like giant ceramic buttons waiting to be glazed, effectively the obverse of their essential miniature nature. She comments that she took inspiration from her own grandmother's collection but that the subversion made the plates seem new and cutting-edge, rather than sentimental.

Lord Chesterfield explains in a letter to his son about the foolishness of fashion yet wishes him to understand the importance of dressing 'according to his rank and way of life':

> ... the fop values himself upon his dress; and the man of sense laughs at it, at the same time that he knows that he must not neglect it.

(19 November 1745)

In the second half of the eighteenth century fine dress begins to be associated with the essentially feminine or effeminate, and a man of good morals will have to dress fashion-appropriately, but quietly. It is now women's clothes that begin to take centre stage. Men become discreet. Artists such as François Boucher, Jean-Baptiste-Siméon Chardin and Jean-Honoré Fragonard begin to paint women with richly jewelled, deliberately showy buttons.

The Baroness Edmond lived in a faux French château, Waddesdon Manor in Buckinghamshire, and the bulk of her collection is French, mostly bought from Parisian dealers. It must have been easy to imagine herself a French aristocrat, in one of her elaborate outfits, taking a turn round the formal gardens, like Marie Antoinette at Versailles. The collection brought her intimately in touch with this imaginary world, but it is a world that demonstrates a certain correspondence with the new ideas of the Enlightenment.

This shift in cultural life across Europe brought about a questioning of institutions, customs and morals. If these were undergoing major change, how could a humble button come into the story? Bachaumont's *Memoirs* (1786, cited in Ginsberg, 1977) compare button making to 'un travail d'imagination ... un texte de conversation inépuisable' ('a work of imagination ... an inexhaustible subject for conversation'). Those who wished the new guiding principles to govern every aspect of their lives might wish to consider even decisions about clothes as an opportunity to behave rationally. On the one hand are the themes that could be illustrated on buttons. On the other, the manufacture of the button was influenced by scientific discovery, using new techniques of production, and foreign exploration supplied new source materials as well as subject matter.

The visitor to Waddesdon notices an array of prettily coloured ornate old buttons, all much the same size, a little dulled with age. But when examined more closely they are of great variety in theme and material. You have to peer into the case, and even then the protective museum lighting means they glimmer like dusty treasure. I was handed a paddle with all the buttons sketched and inventoried, but what I really wanted was to remove them, like a miser, to some private place and handle them, feel how heavy they were, look at their tiny illustrations in more detail.

Many of these buttons suggest the newfound interest in the idea of the natural world, in animals, birds, flowers and landscape. Some of the most unusual are 'Habitat', or *à la Buffon*, buttons, with minutely accurate birds fashioned from snippets of feather and the foreground from moss, all set against a landscape of trees painted on wax and framed in copper. Another set, minutely engraved in silver, after the same Georges-Louis Leclerc Buffon's *Histoire Naturelle, Générale et Particulière* (1749–88), show animals and birds again. Some depict flowers, and they are specific flowers rather than more generic forms – though lacking the finely detailed accuracy of Japanese studies (see Chapter 7). In the Waddesdon collection there are men on horseback, jousting knights, hunting scenes and gentlemen out riding, each horse and person made individual in a set. A set of women is each escorted by their pet dogs, a symbol of fidelity.

Jean-Jacques Rousseau advised a return to a more natural or primitive way of living, and is said to have gone so far as to give up the wearing of white stockings and buttons to this end. A belief in truth emerging from the natural world accounts for the popularity of sets of buttons such as those at Waddesdon, depicting flora and fauna. Particularly popular were insects, which often look as if they were not painted at all, but specimens set behind glass. However, despite Rousseau's influence, or arguably because of it, given the device of taming Émile, the wild boy of his *On Education* (1762), nature was something seen as needing to be governed by intelligent man. On the first page Rousseau sets out his precept:

> Everything is good as it leaves the hands of the Author of things; everything degenerates in the hands of man.

Émile is his attempt to show how natural man can survive the corruptions of society, and it seems that even the button held dangers for the innocent. In this context the landscapes of the eighteenth century tend to be manicured rather than portrayed as wilderness. There is a preponderance of domesticated dogs and horses, which are often given pet names. Another example of this desire to rule over nature lies in the new fashion for sport, which was seen as a return to an earlier more physically able and active humanity, influenced by the examples of classical statuary. However, the Waddesdon set of winter sports' buttons, for example, depicting sleigh rides, skating and hunting scenes, seems a somewhat tame versions of wild nature.

This nature was something that should be brought under our control with a tough regime, and the picturesque was to be seen from a human perspective, rather than as independent of refined judgement. An interest in the natural world and the desire to manage it tends to assume a God-centred view of humanity, and even those who were non-believers found it hard to imagine a world where humanity was not central. Thus classically influenced alternatives were seen as either Eden before the Fall, or sinful forms of a natural world.

The new science of the eighteenth century created the possibility of new and better ways of producing buttons and an enthusiasm for new materials. Just as the improved microscope facilitated scientific enquiry, so the greater availability of eyeglasses made it easier to appreciate fine workmanship. An interesting feature of the development of the button in the eighteenth century is the way some new trompe l'oeil products, such as ceramic mother-of-pearl in a metal setting, were at first bought because they were cheaper and more available. Later imitative effects might become a fashion in their own right, reminiscent of more recent initial fashionable preference for, say, Crimplene over wool or white sliced bread compared with a rustic loaf. These products might be cheap and practical, but their fundamental value lay in their being new, and their consumers' need to satisfy a desire to keep pace with the ever-changing world of fashion.

In the late twentieth century there was a popular reversion to a belief in natural materials, so that just as foodstuffs,

cosmetics and 'lifestyles' are promoted, so buttons are a
selling point when they are 'natural abalone', 'natural shell
from the Australian yellow-lipped oyster' or 'hand-hewn,
naturally resourced, rainforest (and possibly ecologically
sourced) polished hardwood'. Less common tags, for ecological or squeamish reasons, are ivory, tortoiseshell and
other animal sources, though leather is somehow sufficiently
dislocated from the abattoir to retain its popularity. There
are concerns about the environmental effects of farming corals, say, yet coral buttons seem to retain their appeal.

Eighteenth-century ideas that encouraged thinking of
childhood as a period different in kind to adult life were in
part romantic, buoyed up by the findings of the new science
and the belief that observation of children's behaviour
might affect adult character. Alphonse Leroy (1742–1816),
a French physician and professor of medicine, is typical
of those who began to consider the study of childhood as
central to our understanding of the human condition:

> Childhood is a mirror in which we can see ourselves
> young and old at the same time. Ah! I told myself, how
> not to love these small creatures who, when we observe
> them, reveal to us the mysteries of our economy and
> our understanding?

(*Médecine Maternelle*, 1803, p. xxii)

A greater understanding of the biological and
emotional development of children was played out in
literature written specifically for children, in the development of ideas about education and even in the way
children were dressed. Previously they had been got up
like miniature adults, but both the notion of innocence as

15. Cherub fishing, eighteenth-century enamel on brass with steel riveting. This example, probably from a waistcoat, combines themes of classicism and rustic sports. The set of country maids, probably nineteenth century, celebrates the romantic notion of a lost and sentimentalized rural way of life where girls are sweet and jolly.

compared with adult culpability, together with a fashion for classical cherubs, began the creeping sentimentalization of childhood that found its apotheosis in the following century. It also helped form the foundation of modern psychology with its central tenet of the child being father of the man.

In *The Centuries of Childhood* (1960/1962) Philippe Ariès describes childhood as something socially and historically constructed, and thus our idea of children as having altered over time. Children in the Middle Ages were not thought of as different from adults, just smaller and less physically and intellectually able, and thus inferior. In the sixteenth and seventeenth centuries Ariès describes a 'coddling period' where childhood began to be viewed as innocent and sweet, and in reaction a view developed that children might need to be safeguarded and disciplined. Ariès bases much of his theory on his view of seventeenth-century Dutch Old Masters, where on the rare occasions that children do appear, they are male and dressed as small adults. The images of frolicking children on many of the buttons at the Musée de la Mode are evidence of the revolution in how children were seen.

Some of the buttons, showing all the skill and taste of the Parisian ateliers, show episodes from antiquity. One has only to imagine a man – for they were in the main part men – educated in Latin and Greek, at home with the poetry, history and philosophy of the ancient world. Such a man might embark on the Grand Tour in his youth, to see for himself the statues and architecture of Rome, in particular. There was a belief that the eighteenth century might bring about the second coming of classical Rome, though this was not the first occasion of this fantasy. In *The Decline and Fall of the Roman Empire* (Edward Gibbon,

1776), Europe was directly compared with the classical world as 'one great republic'. Whereas previously an educated man might have assumed that truth issued from Christianity, or the codes and mores of his particular local culture, now he was encouraged to take pride in his individuality and how he stood within a common human nature.

An example of this break with moral tradition is the idea of the noble suicide, which was a motif commonly illustrated on buttons. Dante describes the Sorrowful Kingdom where suicides, denied human form, are condemned to live as trees, in perpetual torment as fierce harpies pick off their leaves, one by one (Canto XIII). For the student of the classical world the concept of Christian sin came under question. He might believe, in principle at least, only what could be backed up with empirical evidence and that his opinions should be grounded in his own experience. In this context the button can be seen as a complex *parole*[1], so just as Samuel Johnson likens the use of classical quotation to a sort of password for the literary man (James Boswell, *The Life of Samuel Johnson*, 1791) so the carefully chosen button could represent for the wearer a badge of belonging to that new Age of Reason. Such a man might want his buttons to be illustrated with scenes from antiquity. The nature of the illustrations might seem to grant intellectual refinement.

The artist Ann Carrington noticed such intrinsic value being given to the button in Zulu culture. During a visit to South Africa she was struck by the way objects we happily discard are valued and reused, safety pins becoming elegant brooches, but not in any self-conscious punk sense. They are valued as beautiful objects in themselves rather than as a commentary on their original use. Indentations hammered into a tin can become honoured ornamentation. In particular, she remembers a chieftain's headdress that was surmounted, in pride of place, by a large plain button. In parallel, to the follower of the Enlightenment the ancient world offered alternative values and ways of seeing contemporary events. You might see yourself as an ancient scholar or valiant warrior; your wife could be depicted as a Roman goddess, your children as frolicking cherubs, the offspring of the god of love.

The French Revolution could be seen in terms of classical heroism, and the ideas that interested you could be represented in the narratives that your buttons might relate, such as the Battersea enamel factory in London, founded by Stephen-Theodore Janssen in 1753, which produced transfer-decorated enamels, and the Staffordshire Wedgwood Jasperware displayed at Waddesdon, in white relief on blue, showing elegant deities. The medallions were sometimes mounted in steel by the Wedgwood factory, but more often they were purchased and set in their elaborate mounts by the great steel manufacturers, such as Matthew Boulton of Birmingham, or companies such as Vernon and Hasselwood of Wolverhampton and Woodstock, or Green and Vale of Birmingham. Wedgwood Jasperware was successfully exported to France and Germany in particular. The Waddesdon set depicts a symbol of victory, the crown of laurel leaves, and micro mosaic buttons offer miniature depictions of classical scenes. The faceted steel settings were time-consuming to produce and therefore costly. Such buttons would have been made almost entirely for show, to display the spending power and culture of their wearer, for at the end of the eighteenth century gentlemen's coats were worn open over a matching waistcoat, which bore smaller matching buttons.

16. Josiah Wedgwood and Sons, 1785–1800. Jasper from
Etruria and steel mounts from Birmingham. Made for a man's
formal coat, the larger buttons entirely decorative, worn open
over a waistcoat with smaller-sized matching set.

Classicism may be depicted through the button as sober-minded and portentous, to do with a longing for the ideals and values of the past. Conversely, it may relate to the simplicity of an imagined classical idyll, and often evokes an atmosphere of erotic playfulness. Waddesdon has cameo buttons depicting Cupid wrestling with a lion, to demonstrate love conquering mere physical strength and others show him frolicking with his playmates.

Because of the growth in patronage, many would-be artists started their careers by painting buttons, sometimes with their own original work, but more often copying more established artists. One such example at Waddesdon is the set of Italianate landscapes that may have been painted by J. B. Isabey, the famous portraitist of Napoleon, amongst others. Many larger canvasses were miniaturized, such as the *verre églomisé* landscapes, possibly by C. J. Vernet, using an ancient technique revived by the picture framer Glomy. The method involves painting onto the underside of glass in order to create a sense of luminous depth. Marie Antoinette's painted views on ivory buttons were given to the Duc de la Rochefoucauld-Liancourt, and inspired many another amateur dauber.

Another technique in evidence in the Baroness's collection is the *en grisaille* sequence depicting the divinities: Neptune, Mars and Ceres. This method used a subtle palette of shades of grey, imitating the carved relief of cameos. Also in evidence are *ajouré* buttons with more abstract designs, where the mother-of-pearl has been carved into an openwork pattern resembling lace. Additionally, there was a fashion for silhouettes, initiated by Étienne de Silhouette, the finance minister of Louis XV.

Most of the techniques mentioned here issued from France, but the English innovation of polished steel formed the foundation of the Birmingham trade, of which the poet John Home said, 'it seems as if God had only created men for making buttons' (cited in Ginsburg, 1977). The manufacturer John Taylor was overtaken by his rival Matthew Boulton, who refined the polishing process, which had made steel such a labour-intensive product. Even so it remained an expensive material, 140 buttons selling in 1778 for the then outlandish sum of 142 guineas. The steel was produced in beads that were then either faceted like rose diamonds or flattened into discs. It oxidized easily so could not be worn in wet or damp weather without danger of rust, and thus creates difficulties for the collector. Nevertheless, or perhaps partly on account of this impracticality, they were wildly fashionable, and a 1777 cartoon shows a lady dazzled by the glare from a popinjay's large coat buttons. 'I am the thing – Dem me', he declares. Another contemporaneous anecdote concerns the Baron de Frenilly, who is reputed to have been popular at the gaming table on account of his shiny steel buttons, which reflected his hand for his fortunate opponents.

Whilst the Continent, and particularly France, continued to excel in the finest of handmade buttons produced in specialist ateliers, the factories of Birmingham, according to Adam Smith, began to dominate the world market.[2] The ceramic button was produced by many of the great porcelain factories of Europe: Meissen, Sèvres (in small quantities; many are imitations in fact made in Paris), Capodimonte, Vezzi, in Bavaria, Ludwigsburg, Vienna, Nymphenburg and Berlin, at Vincennes, Delft, and with enamels from Limoges and along the Rhine and Meuse and from Russia. Often buttons were produced as by-products and it was left to the specialist master button makers to complete the process. In England, in particular at Battersea, Chelsea, Worcester, Leeds, Staffordshire, Stoke-on-Trent and Derby, the process was more specifically orientated towards button production and became increasingly more highly mechanized and able to produce ever greater numbers. Just as the faux cameos could be made en masse, in like manner Bohemian handmade glass techniques were adapted by Apsley Pellatt for major production, in parallel with the development of crystal ceramics, known as sulphides.

There remained, for the richest clients, the cachet of hallmarked silver or gold, rare tortoiseshell, glazed beetles, precious stones and diamonds from the New World, amber from the Old. Materials that are in Quentin Bell's terms, 'difficult to obtain and laborious to produce' (1976, p. 31). While a changing society could enjoy the effect of gold and silver in thin layers of foil or brilliantly cut paste jewels, the underlying impression that many hoped to make remained that of being seen as an authentically lavish consumer. In this context it is interesting to consider platinum, a metal of the highest value, higher than gold, yet which never succeeded as an object of consumer desire. Arguably its silver-like appearance would always mask its true value to the observer. It is not until our own time that the idea of rarefied consumption has been turned on its head.

At its most sublime, the eighteenth-century button, like a rebus puzzle, reveals not so much Johnson's notion of language being the dress of thought (*Life of Cowley*, 1779), but that, for the Enlightenment, dress, and thus the button, is the language of new ideas. As capitalism takes hold, new opportunities arise for mass production and the button becomes both more freely available throughout society and is evidence of the seismic changes that continue to rule us. Dorothy L. Sayers used the idea of mass production as a metaphor for our relationship to God, but it also might suggest that even a mass-produced button can have individual value:

> A million buttons, stamped out by machine, though they may be exactly alike, are not the same button.
>
> (D. L. Sayers, *The Mind of the Maker*, 1941, ch. 2, The Image of God)

As the age of industrialization began to take hold, the button became available to a far greater swathe of society in Europe and the United States. Where previously all buttons save those made from fabric off-cuts would have been beyond the means of the majority, cheaper mass-produced buttons seem to have coincided with affluent male dress becoming increasingly less sumptuous.

CHAPTER FOUR

Gentlemen Prefer Buttons

Mr Toots was one blaze of jewellery and buttons

(Charles Dickens, *Dombey and Son*,
1846–8, ch. 14)

As Europe ratcheted into the nineteenth century to the sound of the new monster machines of industry, men who dressed with gorgeous abandon were becoming more and more marginalized. If the entrepreneur wanted to get on, clothes and their buttons were still a perfectly portable opportunity to display wealth and status. However, the trouble was that splendid buttons had begun to make a man look shallow, too concerned with trivia, when really he should be engrossed in scholarship and/or making his fortune, with forceful serious endeavour. The heroes were no longer the great monarchical dynasties, the aristocracy or even the devil-may-care adventurer. Money was the way to get ahead and, in theory at any rate, anyone with a sensible eye to profit margins and emerging capitalist practice might acquire the stuff.

Men of means might still wear expensive buttons, as long as they were sensible enough to be discreet. It was ostentation that was dangerous for the male who wished to enjoy sartorial respect. There might be satisfaction in the rarefied pleasure of knowing that a fine detail of tailoring or subtlety in your so elegant buttons might be noticed by those who sought and paid for a similar effect, but the man of quiet good sense needed to impress society at large. His buttons should not demand attention, in case it looked as if he were too anxious for reassurance, recalling Lord Chesterfield's advice to his son for moderation in such matters.

Luckily for the button industry, there remained other possibilities for conspicuous consumption. If the general impression of his dress needed to become more sombre, there might be opportunities for wearing buttons that, though discreet, might display scenes of a previous age's idea of bucolic revelry and have on one's dressing gown, say, an elaborate eighteenth-century-style paste border. One might enjoy showing off pornographic buttons, discreetly worn on a waistcoat, to the fellows at one's club (see Chapter 8). More innocently perhaps, a man might be given a set of colourful novelty buttons such as the 'Comforts of Married Life', illustrated with images of pipe, slippers, tobacco jar, key to the home, cocoa and a comfortable armchair.

Now that military and naval uniform was distinct from mufti, rank and status could be denoted by fine buttons appropriate to all the intricacies of the services. Relatively low-ranking officers with handsome incomes might still employ a fashionable tailor and have their buttons fashioned out of more expensive materials than their superiors, but since they had to look the same as the standard wear, the practice seems to have been a diminishing one.

Braces began to be worn from the late eighteenth century, at first two simple leather straps, one over each shoulder and attached to a single button on each side, front and back, holding up the new slim-line breeches. Since these were hidden from general view, they could be elaborate and sometimes risqué. Into the nineteenth century they became increasingly fancy, and it was common for a fiancée or wife to fashion a pair of woollen Berlin work or silk embroidery double-tongued braces, though this seems to have coincided with the trouser buttons to which they were attached becoming more sober. R. S. Surtees describes a certain marquis as wearing:

> ...his pea-green cashmere coat lined with silk...displaying his embroidered braces, pink rowing shirt and amber-coloured waistcoat.

> (*Hillingdon Hall*, 1844, ch. 22)

In the nineteenth century special costumes for existing and new sporting activity provided men with further opportunities to dress up, while generally these might be held to be within the bounds of understated dress, even if they had perhaps no intention of actually taking part in such sports. To some extent this stems from a sense of dislocation from an old rural life, fostering a nostalgic desire to be associated with outdoor or country pursuits. Thackeray lampooned those who attempted to take on the authentic dress of working men in the cause of venery and other sporting styles, decrying them as:

> ...violent sports-dresses such as one sees but too often in the parks and public places on the backs of

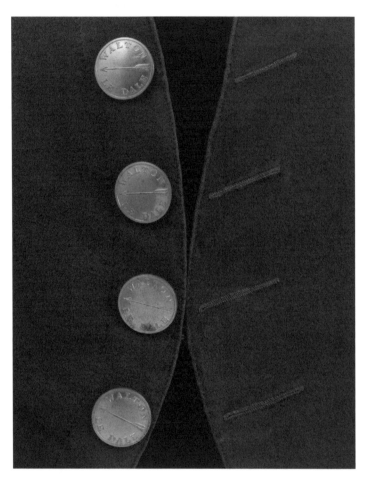

17. Archery coat, 1830–50, green broadcloth fastened with gilt brass buttons, engraved with an arrow, denoting membership of the Walton le Dale Club, Lancashire.

misguided young men. There is no objection in the ost-
ler wearing a particular costume, but it is a pity that a
gentleman should imitate it. I have seen in like manner young fellows at Cowes attired like the pictures we
have of smugglers, buccaneers and mariners in Adelphi
melodramas.

(*Sketches and Travels in London*: *On Tailoring*, 1856)

It was not a question of taking part in a sport so much
as dressing for it. Thackeray satirizes this manner of status
play in *The Yachting Man*:

...you perceive by the bright buttons on his blue coat,
which have a crown and some inscription upon them,
that he belongs to one of the Royal Yacht Club, while
the same bright buttons with the same crown and
anchor, etc., only a size smaller, adorning his waistcoat,
tell you he is not ashamed of it...

(*The Comic Almanack: People One Meets in Society*,
1847, Vol. 2)

Fine buttons were still required for ceremonial dress
– domed brass, silver-gilt, silver and gold, imprinted with
royal coats of arms and the crown – among courtiers,
Members of Parliament and other official roles such as
civic officers and court staff. In Chapter 6 there will be
further reference to the political role buttons came to play
in the French Revolution and its aftermath in particular,
and in Chapter 10 to the American War of Independence
and the growth of the political button and subsequently the
button-badge.

Buttons with political import were popular among the limited electorate of the late eighteenth century in Britain, being worn in sets, sometimes on both jacket and waistcoat. One set of small lithograph buttons has portraits of English political figures and government representatives: Keir Hardie, Haldane, Balfour, Ure, Joynson-Hicks and F. E. Smith, such a mixed set suggesting an interest in political diversity. In 1789 buttons were worn bearing the motto 'Long live the King' to mark George III's recovery from serious illness and to commemorate the Golden Jubilee of George III and Queen Charlotte in 1809. Throughout the nineteenth century, buttons became more overtly political, yet sometimes a particular allegiance might only be present as a discreet 'backname', as for example with flat gilt buttons to celebrate the defeat of Napoleon by the British at Waterloo in 1815, where the reverse of the blank face bore the word 'Wellington' with a wreath of laurel, it being thought more gentlemanly not to be too blatant in such matters.

In the eighteenth century the distinction between fashion and the political button was not clearly differentiated, and, as with fashion, only a small sector of society was involved in purchasing expensive sets of buttons in support of a particular political grouping. One of the earliest known American political buttons of 1776 commemorates the last speech of William Pitt the Elder in the House of Lords, when Pitt spoke out passionately for the American colonists fighting for independence, and refers to the unfairness of their being taxed without being represented in parliament. It bears a raised profile of Pitt and the words 'No Stamp Act'.

In Ireland the political button comes into its own, signifying the complexity of the country's various factions, so that, for example, a button to advocate the repeal of the union with England has on one side an Irish harp and shamrocks, but this nationalist message is modified by 'Repeal of the Union' and 'God Save the Queen', side by diplomatic side, to make clear that Home Rule would not break all ties with the British monarchy. Another eighteenth-century button celebrates the accession of William and Mary in 1688 and a nineteenth-century example of the Battle of the Boyne in 1690, shows William of Orange on a horse.

The new police forces required buttoned uniforms to assert their authority. The variety of these buttons is very great, but to give some idea, Hughes and Lester (1981) show 48 American city police buttons in brass, each based on the particular city or state seal, or embossed with symbols of local industry, mostly worn between 1870 and 1900. The Fire Services, too, each might have their own distinct buttons. Moreover, a man could look to his chattels: his servants, his children and his dependent women. What had been the dress of the affluent man in the eighteenth century curiously became the garb of servants and flunkies in the nineteenth, and even today the dress of the courts and of porters, bellboys and doormen of grander hotels are still resplendent in the manner of eighteenth-century gentlemen. Our man of sense, in paying for his servants' costumes, would have an onlooker declare, 'this man is modest, egad...yet how much must he possess if even his lowly stableman is kitted out in such dashed finery! How bulging must be his coffers if even his kitchen boy wears brass buttons, emblazoned with his monogram or (newly acquired) coat of arms'.

Clubs and organizations such as the Freemasons also had their own buttons that those in the know could recognize. Buttons might be a secret sign of belonging or something to be envied by those who were not yet able to join themselves, thus increasing the cachet of those who were.

Thackeray was a novelist fascinated by the instability of fashion and what it can reveal about a person. He wrote widely about social pretensions for Punch in *The Snobs of England* (1847), and in his novel *The History of Pendennis* (1848–50), in particular. Whenever information is given in these works about the appearance or indeed character of a male character, more often than not it includes something about that character's buttons, until one comes to realize they form a manner of sign system. At the outset of the novel, Major Arthur Pendennis, uncle to the hero, 'a man of active, dominating, and enquiring spirit' and 'military man *en retraite*', is dressed in the height of elegance:

> ... in the best blacked boots in all London, with a checked cravat that was never rumpled until dinner time, a buff waistcoat which bore the crown of his sovereign on the buttons, and linen so spotless that Mr Brummell himself asked the name of his laundress ...

> (Thackeray, 1848–50, ch. 1)

In contrast, we meet young Mr Foker, a very different sort of 'swell', lacking the Major's refinement and breaking the time-honoured rule of fine dressing, that one should avoid seeming to be dominated by the clothes one wears. He is obsessed with show and unable to resist extravagance, dressing ludicrously beyond his years and accompanied by a suitably fashionable trophy pet:

> He had a bull-dog between his legs, and in his scarlet shawl neckcloth was a pin representing another

bull-dog in gold: he wore a fur waistcoat laced over with gold chains; a green cut-away jacket with basket-buttons, and a white upper-coat ornamented with cheese-plate buttons, on each of which was engraved some stirring incident of the road or the chase; all of which ornaments set off this young fellow's figure to such advantage, that you would hesitate to say which character in life he most resembled, and whether he was a boxer en goguette, or a coachman in his gala suit.

(Thackeray, 1848–50, ch. 3)

It was Beau Brummell (1778–1840), forerunner of the plainly suited gentleman, who set a fashion for dark, elegant, apparently simple, in the sense of being understated, but beautifully tailored clothes, with full-length trousers, elaborate cravat (a forerunner of the tie) and no apparent wig. He set a new fashion for washing and changing his linen every day. Brummell is said to have cautioned that 'if people turn to look at you in the street, you are not well dressed'. Buttons were worn smaller and Brummell and his followers eschewed the use of jewels and excessive trimmings. His sense of apparent prudent refinement was taken up by many of his generation, from Lord Byron, with his 'certain exquisite propriety', to the Prince Regent, and in more decadent, colourful form, Oscar Wilde. Despite this seeming simplicity, Brummell claimed it took him five hours to dress and that he had his boots polished with champagne. For an arbiter of new fashion the dandies, as they were called, needed to establish themselves in the common imagination. Richard Dighton caricatures Brummell in 1805 in plain double-breasted jacket with gilt buttons and an expression of careless ease about him.

18. Prince of Wales's drawers, embroidered with his signature feathers, from the nursery at Windsor Castle, once worn by Albert Edward, Queen Victoria's eldest son. 1848–50.

In *Pendennis*, young Pen wants to cut a fine figure, too, yet despite his youthful intemperance, as he gains more economic independence, he never evokes the ridicule Foker's love of fine clothes achieves. At school, Pen is impressed with a fellow pupil who is said to keep a horse in livery, 'and might be seen driving any Sunday in Hyde Park with a groom with squared arms and armorial buttons' (Thackeray, 1848–50, ch. 2). Rebounding from university, he arrives home in smart new clothes and his mother is proud to observe his 'wonderful shooting jackets' (note the plural here, even though there is no mention of his actually shooting anything), 'with remarkable buttons' (ch. 19). Even as he is profligate, we are shown that he has moral worth of a sort. When he has to quit Boniface College with huge debts, Pen is 'reported' to feel remorse and pawns all that he has of value to make partial repayment, except for 'two old gold sleeve buttons, which had belonged to his father' (ch. 20), to a picture framer – who, by the way, just happens to have a charming daughter, which may throw doubt on the purity of his motives. A young man about town, Pen is 'dandified, supercilious, with a black crepe to his white hat, and jet buttons in his shirt front', in a pastiche of Brummell, jet being both expensive and yet suitably restrained. His self-confidence still seems to set Pen apart from people such as Foker. Even when Foker is in romantic distress, his clothes and buttons make him ridiculous rather than pitiful, even infantile perhaps:

> When Pen was gone away, poor Henry Foker got up from the sofa, and taking out from his waistcoat – the splendidly buttoned, the gorgeously embroidered, the work of his mamma – a little white rosebud ...

> (Thackeray, 1848–50, ch. 46)

The idea of childhood as a separate stage in life, together with the concept of the purity of the primitive state, meant that youth was beginning to be thought of as having a close connection with nature and natural goodness. Children needed to be dressed in an appropriately sentimental fashion to demonstrate this essential difference from adults. This is typified in the nostalgic watercolour illustrations of Kate Greenaway in the late nineteenth century, although it is interesting to note that her children's faces retain an idealized, but sometimes disturbingly adult mien. With their doe eyes and sweet but fixed expression they seem oddly poised, even when dressed in the simpler fashions of the turn of the nineteenth century and before.

Children began to be dressed in skeleton suits from around the 1790s, and this fashion for trousers buttoned onto jackets survived for 40 years. Sometimes they were buttoned over each shoulder, in ornamental rows, with the trousers thus rising high. If sufficiently tight, this fashion, intended to be comfortable and practical, tended to impede movement, and getting dressed and undressed again could not be done without assistance. Charles Dickens describes his own such suit as giving 'his legs the appearance of being hooked on just under the armpits' (*Sketches of Boz*, 1838–9, ch. 6). High-buttoned boots and gaiters also relied upon the ministrations of a nursemaid. It is plausible that the business of being buttoned into clothes by servant, or even by one's mother, is one of the underlying causes of the affection we may feel, reminding us of a time when our needs were so assiduously met. Little Paulina, in Charlotte Brontë's *Villette*, tries to do without the help of her maid, which Lucy recognizes as a determinedly brave attempt to prove her independence now that she had been orphaned:

19. Watercolour on ivory of a boy, possibly Sir Frederick
Augustus d'Este, 1794–1848, by Richard Cosway. The buttoned
skeleton suit demonstrates new attitudes towards children – or
children of a certain privileged class – who should, for example,
enjoy more freedom of movement in their dress.

Evidently she was little accustomed to perform her own toilet; and the buttons, strings, hooks and eyes, offered difficulties ...

(Charlotte Brontë, *Villette*, 1853, ch. 1)

Children were dressed in versions of adult costume, such as the military-style tunic worn by Tadzio, the exquisite object of desire in the film of Thomas Mann's *Death in Venice* (1912) – with a row of gilt buttons up to the neck and along the cuffs.[1] Van Eyck's *Children of Charles I* of 1637, where the future Charles II stands central and resplendent in buttoned red velvet, influenced Thomas Gainsborough's *The Blue Boy* of 1770. Frances Hodgson Burnett, in her novel of 1886, went on to condemn many a child to velvet knickerbocker'ed Little Lord Fauntleroy suits, all requiring not only velvet cut-away jackets and lace ruffles but ornate buttons to boot. Alison Lurie makes the point here that Oscar Wilde's aesthetic style of dress owes a great deal to the Fauntleroy look, caricatured in similar knee breeches, with a flower in his buttonhole during a lecture tour of America.

Lurie describes how children's clothes often developed out of versions of adult sports' costume (1981, p. 45). As sports clothes have gradually become less buttoned, and more reliant on stretchy fabrics that do not necessarily require fastening, the tendency has partly reversed, as the elderly take on the romper suits, trews and soft pull-on shoes of toddlers. This trend spread still further in the 1990s, so that it was possible to see men and women of all ages and income groups in comfortable pastel jersey track suits at home and about their everyday lives, with not a button to be seen. The *Guardian* newspaper noted the return to popularity of the shell suit among older men in the news, 'Lockerbie bomber Abdelbaset al-Megrahi... Fidel Castro... you can see the attraction... They have no annoying buttons' (25 August 2009).

Once the nineteenth century had progressed enough for the majority of affluent men in Europe and America to realize that it was safest to be dully dressed, then the nuances between man and man become subtler, and in this context the button alone is less easy to read. Plain dark buttons are much the same on a modest clerk who buys cheap off-the-peg and a lord with a personal tailor. Such buttons do not disclose their wearer's financial means and they allow men a certain mysterious – and some women might say enviable – anonymity. Ever since, what one happens to be wearing exposes women in a way that no longer threatens men. In modern times, women gain status from how they are seen, and thus choosing what clothes to wear can become a minefield. In this context, a Dolce & Gabbana shirt, resplendent with its trademarked buttons, may be worn to denote one's taste and spending power, but may read as vulgar consumerism to some. I may wear a dress of the buttoned-up milkmaid variety, hoping to appear both feminine and fashionable, then glimpse my reflection and realize that I look merely homely. It is rare for men to suffer the same level of anxiety over what they wear because generally they do not define their status in terms of how they are seen by others.

The shift in sumptuous dress from men to women was encapsulated by Thorstein Veblen's concept of vicarious consumption. If men chose not to risk making themselves ridiculous or feminized, then they needed to find a surrogate. A man could express his wealth vicariously through his wife and dependent women. The Victorian era, viewed

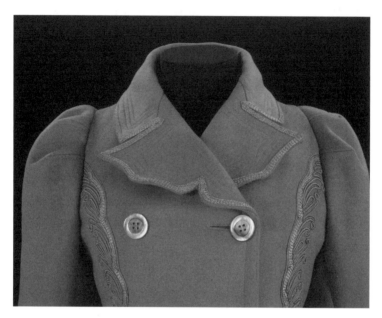

20. Woman's Transformation Suit: double-breasted reefer jacket in grey wool boxcloth, 1892–1897. Masculine tailoring betrayed by fancy revers and applied Russian braid – but simple manlike shell coat buttons.

through its portraiture, shows women in colourful (later dark) outlandish shapes of crinoline and bustle, with their menfolk in the background, substantially built, dark, straight-backed, often bearded, all looking very much the same. Even where women's fashion was thought of as more masculine, the fashions that were popular harked back to conspicuous display. The Directoire dresses of the 1880s, the bodice of which was styled on French revolutionary male apparel, had large buttoned-back revers and deep cuffs, completely at variance with their modestly dressed contemporary consorts. Revers, or the turned back lining of a jacket, had been an opportunity from the mid-1860s for some measure of decoration on otherwise sombre men's apparel. Such revers had originally been designed as practical campaign wear: to allow a jacket longer life, as after the revers became dirty they could then be buttoned back to reveal the clean facing, the food-spattered surface thus hidden from view.

Nineteenth-century women's clothes became increasingly buttoned up, particularly in Britain under the influence of Queen Victoria, so that even a nursing mother would have vertical slits tailored into her dress, fastened with buttons on either side, for not-so-easy access.

Early in the century Birmingham manufacturers stopped using simple hand tools and the unsophisticated hand-powered machines that had been used to supplement the functions of early machinery. In 1794 Ralph Heaton patented a machine for the production of button shanks that was steam-powered and inexpensive to use. In 1851 his machines made nearly 750,000 shanks. In 1801 the Jacquard loom began to produce fabric that could cover buttons with a convincing version of the time-consuming handmade silver thread and purl (metal thread wound into a short coil) passementerie of the seventeenth and eighteenth centuries. Machines could mete out ribbons of printed images, or textilographs, which could quickly and cheaply give the impression of the skilled painter or copyist. Benjamin Sanders Junior made affordable fabric buttons more practical with his invention of a flexible fabric shank that made buttons easier to wash, as an earlier problem with rusting could then be avoided. Much of former ages' household pewter came to be melted down and fashioned into inexpensive buttons – and, incidentally, thereby making domestic pewter a rarer and therefore more highly sought-after commodity in today's antique trade.

In 1867 Alexander Parkes exhibited the first cellulose nitrate based plastic, called Parkesine, which was used for various objects including false teeth, combs, billiard balls and, of course, the button (Haldane, 2007). In the 1870s celluloid was developed to imitate ivory, tortoiseshell, marble, horn, and so on – the forerunner of today's plastics. The more specialized the machines became, the more efficient and the less easy it was for small-scale producers and crafts to compete. Once these old crafts were no longer practiced, their skills were largely forgotten, so that in any large-scale commercial sense, there was no turning back.

By the 1880s the many new industrial processes and the availability of cheap, including child, labour from the countryside, created a wide variety of buttons at affordable prices. However, if industrialization was taking over, then increased standardization would eventually give way to some measure of counter tendency. This was expressed through a renewed appetite for luxury one-off 'artisan' production, typified by the Arts and Crafts Movement. In fact many of these new craft workers were drawn from artistic circles, rather than from the original practitioners.

The medical dangers of tight corseting on women, together with the aesthetic critics of dress, provided a brief period of greater simplicity in women's fashions. Women wore their hair long and loose and their dresses were medieval in style, often accompanied by unstructured flowing capes and shawls, as in many Pre-Raphaelite paintings. Fortunately for the button, this movement was short lived, though its spirit has survived in the loose female garb of the hippy movement, and more recently in manifestations of New Age and some grunge styles.

We are not all hot on the heels of fashion. Often people stick to a trend they feel particularly suits them or that reminds them of a time when they felt at least more at ease with themselves. At school I recall a lay teacher who must have been young in the fifties and fancied herself perhaps an Ava Gardner or Marilyn Monroe, for she was fair and had a way of pouting. She carried a little weight, but somehow maintained a tiny waist – and it was before the days when a lady might consider dying her hair, at least in the provinces, so that her greying locks were crimp-waved to her shoulders and she wore pebble-lensed glasses. She must have decided that navy blue and deep brown were teacherly, but in all other respects she dressed as a college girl from the romantic films of her youth: in baby-hued twin-sets whose buttons she would check to make sure they were correctly fastened. In the summer term she wore matching pencil or sunray pleated skirts that kicked up as she walked. Her plump torso was supported by extravagantly lovely legs. I remember her in permanent blush, no doubt aware of our sly gaze. I thought her ludicrous, but now she strikes me as brave as any emperor. These proclivities in many of us, when taken to relative extremes, can create as much comedy or grounds for contempt as that of which up-to-date fashion is more often accused. One's clothes can betray an unwillingness to face or lack of interest in the future both then and now, and even express a romantic soul.

The sense of what is or is not appropriate may cover a wide range of styles, but nonetheless, like common sense, many of us tend to feel we have more than the average competency. One might declare, 'I may not have a sense of what is fashionable, or even what suits me, but I do understand that what you are wearing is quite wrong – embarrassingly ill-judged, in fact'. Depending upon the average, eventually watered-down fashions of any period, something buttoned to the neck, say, may seem absurdly uptight or even a signpost to some mental disorder; at the other extreme it may suggest appropriate formal wear, as in a man's modern business suit or merely a deliberately finessed counterbalance to a dress with a very short skirt, or perhaps in exciting contrast to transparent fabric that usurps any apparent primness.

Veblen argues that 'the need of dress is eminently a "higher" or spiritual need' (1994, ch. 14). For the new industrialist moguls of the nineteenth century, churning out mass-produced buttons, and even for the consumer in the poorer strata of society just beginning to be able to purchase such buttons, some of this 'spiritual' need seemed to be evaporating. Yet even when buttons are simple, they seem to retain a place of honour.

While the anti-fashion robes of the Pre-Raphaelites did not survive much beyond the 1880s, women were again taking up the tightly fitted masculine jacket, an echo of the *à la Suzanne*, a century before. Jenny Jerome, the American heiress, is pictured about the time of her marriage to Randolph Churchill in 1874 in a plain, dark, newly fashioned bodice with close-up rows of tiny plain buttons from chin to below the waist and at the cuffs, presaging the *cuirass*, which was worn shorter and even more fitted. Her likeness was much reproduced in the press, gorgeously proportioned, a supreme trophy wife. The Gibson girl, the idealized, hourglass feminine figure of illustrator Charles Dana Gibson, represents this look. Some women might agitate for greater rights and freedoms, but like current-day WAGS, she represented an idealized form of womanhood for many men. No longer gently in the background, but choosing to rein in her obvious intelligence and physical prowess in support of her manly man. Compare this figure with crinolined Dora in Charles Dickens's *David Copperfield*, or even the more capable but gentle and unassuming Agnes, and we see how much the model has evolved. Yet from a political point of view very little has changed, and the role of a woman is still only that of a figurehead.

Meanwhile, on the streets of London, a small but significant movement was gathering force. Pearly Kings and Queens have been more or less consistently sentimentalized in popular culture as the epitome of the cheeky cockney. Generally, they wear dark clothing covered in twinkly buttons topped with a cheery grin, and reassure us that it was fun to be working-class Londoners in the dear 'cor blimey' past. Their style is Edwardian costermonger meets Hollywood. Remember Dick Van Dyck in the Walt Disney film *Mary Poppins*, dancing oh so cheerily to 'Supercalifragilisticexpialidocious', with thumbs akimbo in the lapels of a too short-legged suit and accompanied by a pearly band with their chorus of 'Um diddle diddle diddle um diddle ay'? Another, more recent, jolly chorus of pearlies appeared in *Me and My Girl*, the London West End musical. In *The Ziegfeld Follies* film of 1946, a troupe of quaint pearlies are set in contrast to the elegances of Fred Astaire and Lucille Bremer. The 1963 film *Irma la Douce* again has pearlies, this time incongruously singing away in a Parisian market. They are the nub of jokes, sweet and daft in relation to the gritty protagonist of the film *Trainspotting*, or providing a spot of postmodern irony and proof of class legitimacy for Pete Townsend of the band The Who. Townsend wore a version of a pearly suit for a tour in the 1970s; the White Stripes band dressed up in buttons for the cover of their *Icky Thump* album in 2007. They apparently thought that the title, evoking a colloquial expression of surprise, lent a sense of north country British grit, though ironically this is at odds with their south-east, cockney-pearly costume theme. Even Fozzie Bear from *The Muppets* fancied himself a pearly, performing 'Any Old Iron' with the pop singer Elton John.

Since I had only ever seen pearlies in films or once as a rather lacklustre advertising gimmick in a supermarket (they must have hired the costumes from the local theatre, for they smelt of old sweat), selling meat pies I seem to recall, they seemed alarming, too familiar, too loud – and pearlies in general seem not remotely authentic. Most of those you are likely to come across are not the real thing, yet the notion of authenticity is confusing here. What would an authentic pearly involve? One does not berate actors for not being themselves when acting. A pop singer's attempts as an actor might not impress, a newsreader's opportunity to dance a rumba might not seem sufficiently sensual, but one would be unlikely to accuse them of inauthenticity. In relation to the pearlies, the concern seems to stem from a vague yet reassuring concept of the good and modest poor, and that any attempt to glamorize them somehow undermines this essential innocence. It is not the sentimentality but the sense of success that troubles. Just as small children should not be too aware of their charms or artists be seen to enjoy their success too much, any self-confidence can evoke a puritanical response – at least in the British. It is also worth mentioning that pearlies were almost always sentimentalized in the music halls, often by their own kind. Kate Carney, for example, in her role as the coster comedienne, which stretched from the last years of the nineteenth century to 1950, sang her signature 'Three Pots a Shilling': three pots of flowers remain a popular symbol on pearly garments.

The history of the Pearly Kings and Queens is chronicled by the splendidly named Pearl Binder, in *The Pearlies, A Social Record*. This book tells of the poorest street sellers, or costermongers, vending their wares on foot, and if they were lucky with the help of a donkey – fruit, vegetables, second-hand clothing, kitchen pots and pans – any old iron in fact. It was a trade anyone, however destitute they might be, could turn to. If you had nothing, you could pick up windfall fruit to sell, or anything that might be got, legitimately or otherwise, to earn a few pence. They would call out, often in song, their oysters, cabbages, oranges, vinegar or knife-grinding service. Their competing shouts added to the clamour of London streets. Ben Jonson's character Clerimont describes another as not being able to 'endure a costermonger. He swoons if he hears one' (*Epicene*, 1609, act 1, sc. 1). Costermongers had a reputation for being concerned with money alone:

> Virtue is of so little regard in these costermonger times...

> (William Shakespeare, *Henry IV Part II*, act 1, sc. 2)

Doctor Johnson mentions costermongers in his dictionary as 'costard mongers', describing them as sellers of apples, 'round and bulky like the head'. Sometimes they would bang a pail or drum, literally to drum up trade. In the squalor of the London streets, as the engine of industrialization drove more and more to try and often fail to find work, you might sell a few flowers, an apron of coal fallen from a passing cart, hot potatoes, handmade needlework bits or rough trinkets, boots, offer yourself as rat-catcher, anything to keep you from the workhouse, crime and prostitution, the treacherous world evoked by Hogarth and Gustav Doré.

The fight to survive brought them into conflict with the authorities. Gradually though, many began to take up regular pitches under licence, and some say the need to negotiate between these very poor costermongers and oppressive regulators gave rise to the leaders who became the first Pearly Kings and Queens. They were well established by the late 1850s, though the pearly royalty came later in the 1880s, and pearlies are first mentioned in the *Oxford English Dictionary* as late as 1886. Yet their leadership could have existed without the 'unnecessary' display of buttons. Their behaviour demonstrates why costume, and in this case the button, can sometimes be important to a fragile sense of self-respect. Being small objects easily mislaid by the more affluent, buttons might be picked up from the roads and gutters, or along the muddy shore of the Thames, having been accidentally dropped overboard, like jewels they must have seemed. A moment of aesthetic indulgence in an often harshly hand-to-mouth existence, sewing them onto one's clothes was a declaration of a need for something other than what is strictly necessary for survival – a desire for beauty, for art.

Plate 1. *Shroud for a Colourful Soul*, Jane Burch Cochran, 44" × 66", 2005. Materials: fabrics, bullion beads, sequins, paint, found crotched items, gloves and buttons. Method: hand appliquéd quilted and embellished, machine patchwork and hand tied using buttons.

Plate 2. One of Grayson Perry's fabulous *Claires*, the blue ceramic 'crucifixion' buttons made to go with a skirt decorated with a face of Jesus design.

Plate 3. *Ovuliidae*, map of Paris, signed and sealed, Elisabeth Lecourt. A smart girl's dress fashioned from a map and buttoned up as it should be, 2008.

Plate 4. *Tea for Two*, a textile three-dimensional coffee pot, held together – stabbed through – with buttons, by Priscilla Jones. Mixed media with found objects, 2006.

Plate 5. *Mens Suits*, an installation by Charles LeDray, commissioned and produced by Artangel, 2009. Photograph by Julian Abrams.

Plate 6. *Empty Me*, Ran Hwang, 2009, National Museum of Contemporary Art, Korea, 210 × 540 cm (six panels in all). Buttons pinned on wood panel.

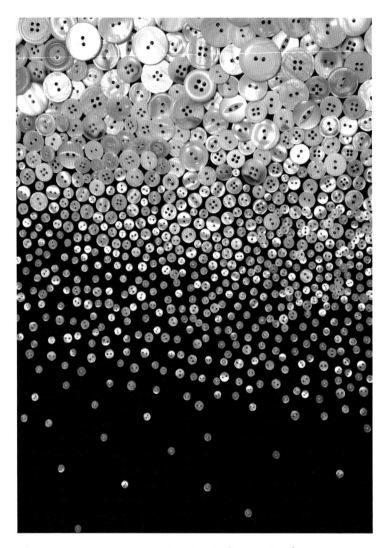

Plate 7. Ann Carrington, detail of *Crown Jewels*, the natural mother-of-pearl buttons in all their subtle variety of shape and colour, shown front and back, like a shimmering constellation.

Plate 8. Zandra Rhodes handmade buttons, with her definitive panache: a hand-embroidered covered button edged with satin pleating used on pleated jacket.

Plate 8 b Queen of Hearts Collection, classic button edged with rhinestones.

Plate 8 c Hand-embroidered with gold gathered edging used on pleated jacket.

Plate 8 d Printed and hand-fringed for African Collection.

One theory to account for their dress suggests that when a ship coming back from Japan washed up its cargo of pearl buttons in the Thames, one of those who scrabbled in the mud for any valuable pickings was a road sweeper, one Henry Croft. Possibly it was excise men who seized the cargo and then sold off the booty cheaply to all comers. Pearl buttons were relatively expensive and out of reach to people like costermongers. However, when Croft came upon such a hoard of buttons he chose not to sell them but to decorate his clothes instead.

An alternative interpretation is that some of the market stallholders already embellished the hems of their wide trousers with rows of buttons, and thus Croft had had the idea of smothering the entire surface of his suit. In the first decades of the nineteenth century clothes would have been gradually handed down through the layers of the class system, so that the very poor were wearing discarded versions of upper-class dress, even including hats and canes. Gradually, top hats would become damaged and begin to take on a deflated appearance. When the upper and middle classes saw the pearlies they would recognize the fashions of their youth perhaps, their clothes having taken some years to filter down, and feel a swell of nostalgia. Pearly Queens wore button decorated hand-me-down battered old Society ladies' hats. Their children too, dressed in the adult styles no longer worn by the fashionable, became decorated miniature versions of people from the past, like many a representation of the Artful Dodger in Charles Dickens's *Oliver Twist* (1838). This tradition continued with only small adjustments to the times, so that one sees family photographs taken in the 1960s with the style of pearly wear hardly changed from 80 years earlier, only the younger women might be incongruously in mini skirts and white patent boots. Today their children may still wear the traditional suit, but are in trainers and caps on back to front, rapper-style.

Croft was an orphan, only five feet tall, and neither drank nor smoked, yet by all accounts he must have possessed considerable charm, dedicating his free time to raising money for the slum dwellers, collecting money in the public houses of the East End. His example encouraged others he worked with to join him in the charitable work. The pearlies helped feed the dock workers striking in 1889, and 40 years later they supported the Welsh miners who came to petition Parliament. Henry Croft himself was a supporter of women's rights and the Suffragist movement, which makes it a strange small irony that the 1964 Disney film *Mary Poppins*, which first introduced the pearlies to many of us, was distressing to P. L. Travers, who had written the original novel. She was shocked to see Mrs Banks, the children's mother, interpreted as a selfish suffragette who eventually comes to her senses by giving up campaigning and returning to the hearth and home, whereas Travers had written her as an admirable early feminist figure.

Pearlies collected mainly from their own neighbourhoods, setting up a tradition of self-help in the community. Before Croft died in 1930, groups of pearlies had been formed across all London boroughs, so that at his funeral over 400 members came to pay their respects to the first Pearly King of Somerstown. It must have been an extraordinary sight to see them in full-buttoned display, accompanied by their donkeys with harnesses and saddles all covered in the pearl button regalia.

In Croft's time the patterns of decoration on the pearlies' costumes gradually became differentiated—and today design has not stagnated since new patterns and even contemporary images are brought in, such as spaceships and mobile telephones. However, Croft preferred his 'smother' effect, covering every surface of his worn-out dress coat, trousers, waistcoat, cravat (or kingsman), boots, top hat and stick. Binder suggests that many of the onlookers would have been manual workers and might well have been impressed by the effort involved marching about in such heavy costumes, shaking their collecting tins, covering the local markets and carnivals. Croft's idea caught on, and soon all his fellow charity workers were adorning their clothes with pearl buttons. It was a considerable task sewing them on, when a man's suit might take as many as 30,000 and a woman's outfit even more.

Partly because of the sheer weight of the smother pattern (as much as three-quarters of a hundredweight), and the expense of so many buttons, pearlies started to develop styles using smaller quantities, and today plastic buttons are sometimes used, being both lightweight and easier to accrue. Incidentally, the British Button Society still regularly contributes buttons to the pearly cause. As the pearlies gained in numbers, different families would come to have their own distinctive patterns, incorporating their names, fancy borders and symbols, driven to create something unique. In time these differences marked out separate pearly territories. A variety of symbols appear, including those for good fortune, involving suits of cards, horseshoes and old boots; signs of fertility such as teapots, flowers, moons, and stars; signs to ward off evil such as the 'eye of God', crossed anchors, crowns, shooting rockets and flying birds. The borders were meant to keep the wearer safe, and the simple circle motif symbolized the sun, the wheel of fortune turning, or perhaps just the wheels of a donkey cart. Some pearlies reckon a circle represents money, some eternity, and others the face of Big Ben. Some have claimed that the motifs spring from pagan images.

The craft skills involved are considerable. Each button had to be sewn on separately, using waxed button-hole thread. Sometimes red-coloured thread was used and more lately nylon. They might be overlapped to create a damask or three-dimensional effect. Ostrich feathers were also popular, dyed a patriotic red, white and blue, in all probability the tattered remnants of some lady's discarded, once fashionable hat. In the twentieth century red bugle beads, known as 'bugs' were included or the pearl buttons themselves were dyed to create contrast. Binder includes a number of touching biographies of notable pearlies, including the Pearly King of West Ham, Bill Davidson, who had been a docker all his life, as well as fighting in both world wars. His designs are some of the strongest, based on a repeated triangular form and worked in delicately tinted identical small buttons. He was also responsible for making his wife and Rover the dog's outfits, and is pictured with a silk kingsman at his neck. These stocks are reminiscent of the eighteenth-century gentleman, usually pale in colour, and worn well into the 1970s by retired dockers.

Today some pearlies still remain, such as Stephanie Jolly, who at the age of 22 is currently the youngest reigning Pearly Queen of Highgate. Her grandparents are the Pearly King and Queen of Crystal Palace. She enjoys collecting for charity but claims she can be the butt of jokes, comparing her image to that of people who dress up as chickens to run the London Marathon. Describing her own outfit as a skeleton suit, she explains that:

...it's hard work. We get the basic suit in a dark colour that fits and has a bit of wear in it. It's nicest in velvet. You lay out the pattern and build it up slowly.

(Marie Jackson, *BBC News*, 2009)

It is impressive how well pearlies have managed to maintain their costumes when these must have been easily damaged, particularly as a superstition grew up that it was lucky to possess a pearly's button. What was it about the button that appealed to so many? Ann Carrington suggests that it might have something to do with the way a button is something unchanging. Like the wheel, it does not need to be improved: it is just itself. Yet again the button is able to express something hard to articulate that appeals to the instinct to cherish and is at the same time reassuringly ordinary.

Commissioned to create a portrait of the British Queen on her eightieth birthday for the Rothschild Collection, Carrington combined the Queen's love of the postage stamp and of buttons with her own interest in the pearlies and their history. A stamp of Elizabeth II was blown up to huge proportions, two metres high, the printed pixels transformed into the separately attached buttons. Carrington uses a rich array of colours, like a patchwork woven across the familiar young profile, the 'stamp's' perforations in brilliantly coloured stripes. Like pearlies' skeleton suit borders, the perforations define and frame the portrait. Perhaps it wards off demons too. Even the first-class stamp symbol becomes a play on the status of the Queen: it is Elizabeth II, but she is in some sense the first, the most important, in being the representative figurehead of her kingdom.

The artwork *The Pearly Queen of Shoreditch* (2005) scintillates in the half-light, hung high up in the restaurant at Waddesdon, a deft acknowledgement of the house's button collection, but as the business of eating carries on below, the domestic, mundane setting seems particularly apt for the medium Carrington has chosen. She reigns in glittering silent isolation above the clatter of cutlery and raised voices.

Carrington has gone on to create further *Pearly Queens*, of *Dalston* and *Hackney Wick*, and other works that also use buttons, such as *Pearly Queen Jewels* and *Union Jack*. She likens the button to a symbol of Western civilization, but she says, with 'a humorous twist'. This sense of wit, and of 'making the holy out of the humdrum' pervades Carrington's work, and, I think, her fascination with the button. She has shelves of jam jars and transparent boxes full of buttons, like sweets in a sweet shop, just waiting for her to assemble them into something that captures her imagination. Significantly, she mentions being attracted to the notion of producing sophisticated versions of childhood ephemera (see Chapter 5).

From the early decades of the nineteenth century the button began to have a more disturbing significance in relation to childhood. Previously, in the so-called cottage industries, children had been part of small-scale button manufacture. All children from poor families would have had to work, and button making was at least indoor work, and was largely given to girls. This continued in much of the rest of Europe, but in England, and America to a lesser extent, children were drawn into the newly mechanized button factories. Small fingers could be useful, and children cost less than adults. Under apprenticeship schemes a manufacturer might get paupers from orphanages and the workhouses, and was required to give them only food and

21. Ann Carrington, *Crown Jewels*, 2010.

shelter, thus saving on the wage bill. Many, including John Wesley (co-founder of the Methodist movement), thought that such indentures might be beneficial in protecting children from youthful idleness and vice, and for some the factories may indeed have meant an improved way of life. By the mid-nineteenth century employment of children under 14 was at its height in Europe and the North American states, but gradually machines were beginning to be more specialized and complicated. The movement to reduce child labour was aided by the need manufacturers had for stronger and more skilled adult male workers. However, today in the button industry children are still at work, in the factories of China (see Chapter 7), sometimes facing hazardous conditions to supply the world market.

In the twentieth century buttons become widely available, and with the spread of Western-style clothing, even in their most modest mass-produced form they can become new status symbols, a familiar pattern in Western culture. The cheapness and availability of buttons also allows a strain of humour and light-heartedness, which might be said to mask the engine of capitalism busy at work. Buttons seem to embody a new and arch interpretation of the world: twentieth-century cuteness has had a profound effect on moral attitudes, on approaches to art and to human nature – all demonstrated through the button.

CHAPTER FIVE

Commerce and Cuteness

...Let's go where I'll keep on wearin'
Those frills and flowers and buttons and bows
Rings and things and buttons and bows.

Buttons and bows, buttons and bows...

In high silk hose and peek-a-boo clothes
And French perfume that rocks the room
And I'm all yours in buttons and bows.

(Song from *Paleface*, with Bob Hope, 1948)

What of the modern, twentieth-century world? The idea of childhood becomes an obsession with youth. After the constraints of hourglass Edwardian fashions, women's clothes become more relaxed for a while. However, before a woman might sigh with relief, dieting becomes the rage, for women had to be able to wear clothes best suited to a pre-pubescent boy. Although the Great War puts a freeze on fashion, the 'mad' 1920s ensues and women are wearing tubular-shaped coats with oversized childish buttons. Alison Lurie comments (1981, p. 74) that the face of a young flapper, framed by her bobbed hair, 'was that of a small child: round and soft, with a turned-up nose, saucer eyes and a pouting "bee-stung" mouth' – the eyes, nose, mouth and face, one might say, of a button. The popular shirt-dresses, cut loose and square, often had rows of tiny buttons at the cuff and down the front, reminiscent of the baby clothes of their infancy. Shoes had the ankle-straps and button fastenings of a toddler's first booties.

Men, too, were beginning to lose some of their gloomy nineteenth-century bulk. Young men of fashion were experimenting with colour and more fitted suits in lighter-weight materials, and a gulf between youth and even early middle age began to open up. A young man, moderately fashionable, might consider wearing, say, a jumper rather than a jacket, sometimes with buttons along the shoulder, as if for a young child. A man of even a few more years, one who had experienced the war, might feel uncomfort-able without the formality of a more uniform-like subdued suit. Although the 1930s reversed this pattern, for women at least, it was to occur again in the cruel age-divide of the 1950s and 1960s.

Cuteness is at the heart of twentieth-century attitudes to consumer goods and lends itself with ease to the dimin-utive button. It is essentially to do with youth and inno-cence, or sometimes childishness and wanton ignorance. Mary Quant, in the 1960s, designed dresses with buttons down the back to suggest both the gamin cute child, and, more subversively, the deliberately childish child-woman who needs adult help to dress and undress. When and why the idea of cuteness crept into our fashion choices is hard to pinpoint, but its influence has infected almost every aspect of aesthetic and moral choice. Even if it is a word one might not use, the sense of what is cute or not has been pivotal in the advertising industry and thus central to successful commerce. Cuteness has a naive charm; it leads one to expect what is small and pretty. Newborn chicks are cute. Babies are said to be cute. Yet calling something cute suggests a youthful and perhaps superficial response and usually refers to superficial qualities. One might be charmed by the cute, but be warily self-conscious enough to dress up such a response as something that seems less potentially embarrassing. Better by far to choose some buttons because 'they are interesting' or as 'they remind me of some buttons in a Fragonard painting in the Frick Collection' or simply because they are the right colour, rather than admit they seem quaint and make one come over all soppy. One might not care what people think, of course, but the point here is that there is something faintly undignified about holding such a view.

The word 'cute' derives from 'acute', suggesting something pointed and far sharper than the air of fluffiness that 'cute as a button' brings to mind. Yet the expression has attached itself with such tough thread that it is sometimes difficult to remember the uncompromising, utilitarian button, and all the other cute-free types associated with war, violence, sex, politics, crime and death. A sense of purity can inhabit the term, and Peter Edwards in his essay on cuteness and related concepts suggests a link with 'cutaneous', that is relating to the skin, as in 'Cuticura', a popular soap first manufactured in 1865.

One of the problems in diagnosing the aura of cuteness that has come to be associated with button-ness, is the confusingly wide variety of things that are sometimes called cute, and that can confound any attempt to mark out areas where the term should not be properly used. Moreover, the wearer of cute buttons is often thought to be invested with that quality. I may be plain yet wear a beautiful dress; I might just become cute or *jolie-laide* in cute buttons.

In Japan, the rebellious, anti-fashion, punk movement of the UK 1980s, transmogrified in the 1990s into mainly young female, white lace punk – a high fashion, peek-a-boo, frilly style, the epitome of cuteness. The wearer seemed to be saying, 'Even when I want to be aggressive, look what happens... I'm so essentially cute I can't help getting it wrong, and here I am being pretty again!' One could also see, lounging on street corners, boys adopting this hybrid form of the punk look, with less flounce, and rather more rips and safety pins to their white lace. Neither gender seemed to countenance any but the whitest cleanest whites. Here there were no dead rats hanging off one's lavatory chain belt, no fetid dreadlocks: safety pins were not worn through an ulcerated cheek, but might be threaded with sequins, beads and cute buttons to act as decorative fastenings. They did wear an appropriately sullen expression, but one which would be automatically dropped as soon as they spoke, even maintaining the polite non-verbal bowing etiquette.

If cuteness is associated with youthful characteristics, it may be that this springs from our response to a 'child's physiognomy (which) instinctively induces feelings of happiness and protectiveness' (Papanek, 1995). Cartoon characters and animals have the same vulnerable features, genderless and timid. As I have suggested above, there is something of a child's face about the button, usually round and small and which can have the same sentimental associations as the pansy, in the language of flowers. The 'face' of a button seems to mimic a childlike drawing of the human face, or the ubiquitous smiley or sulky icon face. The thread holes can suggest two eyes, or nostrils, and when there are four, the thread itself can seem to mimic a human mouth. Even when the button is not round it tends to retain some of this association.

Perhaps the use of buttons in children's games has helped create this cute association. Schoolboys used once to play a game that allotted a set of values to different types of button, rather as in marbles or conkers, known as playing 'sinkies'. Highly valuable were livery buttons, from servants' uniforms, and most sought after were those bearing images of sports or animals. Another game involved asking questions to discover who had hidden a button, recalled as 'Button, button, Who's got the button...' in Robert Frost's poem 'The Witch of Coös' (1923). The game's title acted as a newspaper headline for a post-Second World War US policy of non-fraternization, when one army unit issued button-badges to displaced females in Germany, demonstrating their particular origins with colour-coding, to distinguish them from forbidden *Fräuleins*.

Children might be allowed to play with buttons from their mother's box: they might enjoy ordering them in various ways, creating their own private hierarchy of value. Buttons might be used for a rag doll's eyes or to replace one missing from a soft toy. Young girls in America, between 1860 and 1900, Diana Epstein explains, would collect strings of buttons to act as romantic charms: if they succeeded in reaching 999, then a future husband might be seen. Others might prefer to swoon over images of their favourite film star, set in a celluloid button. Babies might be pacified with a row of leftover buttons, hung over their cots: they could goo and gurgle and clutch the colourful spheres, as they learnt to focus their attention on the outside world – and on the button.

In the early 1970s, Japanese teenagers and young women bought into early cute culture, and an appeal to cuteness became a highly successful marketing tool. Previously the mother–daughter relationship had been a central theme in girls' comics, but there was a shift towards this new infantilizing culture. In 1975 Emperor Hirohito and his wife were pictured looking a little coy beside Mickey Mouse, on a visit to the United States. This image was widely distributed and held to be *kawaii* or cute. The term is also associated with the idea of pity or *kawaiso*. Thus the Japanese premiers were delightfully vulnerable. A new word was coined, *otome-tique*, for that quality in objects and thoughts that was girlish and cute.

Gradually, cuteness became a mainstream approach to merchandising almost all everyday items. Girls at university in the 1990s dressed as little girls, with ankle socks (or knee socks worn loose so that they were continually having to be pulled up, as with a child who hardly knows how to manage) and short skirts; often posing with pigeon toes, they would finger their buttons as if they had difficulty in either buttoning or unbuttoning them without aid.

> Kawaii can refer to various things: clothes, accessories, manners, personalities, feelings, looks, smells, colors, tastes etc... Babies, grandmothers, bald men, crooked faces/teeth, carelessness, dumbness, strawberry or other fruity sweet smells, flatulence, white and pinkish colours, ice cream and candy...
>
> (Kimiko Akita, 'The Sexual Commodification of Women in the Japanese Media', 2005, p. 46)

I have heard Mount Fuji and ear-picks referred to as *kawaii*. The epithet is even more widely used than 'cool' and more lately 'hot' in the West, and is less associated solely with the younger generation. Many of Kimiko Akita's contexts can be directly linked with what is deemed cute in the modern button and are exemplified in two of the most popular Japanese selling stratagems displaying this connection. The button represents something Western, and might offer a way of showing how one would like to be seen, yet it is insignificant enough not to suggest too selfish a degree of anti-social individualism.

The Hello Kitty campaign, or *Kitty-chan* in Japanese, is still popular, involving the ubiquitous white kitten with raised paw. The cat image is said to spring from Chinese folklore *maneki-neko*, as an omen of good luck. The cat's gesture is a traditional beckoning gesture, rather than one of farewell as might be suggested in the West, and statues or posters of the cat are often used to invite customers into shops. Specialist shops sell only Hello Kitty branded merchandise, and of course its image can be found on buttons, in massive quantities: for clothes, for fastening bags and I have seen them also on snow boots, umbrellas, clothes, soft toys and sewn decoratively on the ubiquitous flannels carried in humid weather. One may not wish to be seen with a furry Hello Kitty-shaped mobile phone, but a discreet kitten button on one's cuff or buttoning a purse or a handbag can more subtly suggest the same fundamental vulnerability, and demonstrate the way one is hoping to be seen by others.

The sinuous organic forms of the Art Nouveau movement were inspired in part by a stylized but nature-based asymmetric Japanese aesthetic. Although many such designs are extremely pretty, feminine or enchanting, it would seem odd to refer to them as cute. Many Art Nouveau buttons are slightly irregular in shape, often cast in silver, where the long loose hair of the typical aesthetic woman combines with organic forms. She represents the elements, or perhaps Marianne, the symbol of France. Émile Gallé produced metal-mounted glass buttons, which again relied on organic forms, acid-etched flowers and plants, subtle and restrained. The great European glass factories of Austria and Czechoslovakia made pressed-glass buttons, resembling lacy glass, and though the patterning here is more symmetric, they still demonstrate a new formal freedom, and act as a link with the deliberately hand-tooled, or as Thorstein Veblen deftly has it, the 'honorific crudeness' (1994, p. 97) of buttons of the Arts and Crafts movement.

Even the prevalence of the heart form, or the heart pierced by an arrow, both common motifs of the sentimental cute, somehow suggests here too much sincerity to merit the term. It is as if there has to be some quality of knowing coyness in our relationship to an object for it to be thought of as cute, so that even depictions of fairies, when treated with relative 'realism', seem to fall short. Agents need to be able to distance themselves from any sense of potentially painful emotion for it to be enjoyed as cute. And there is something too human in the character of such fairies, which, like Titania and Oberon in *A Midsummer Night's Dream*, suggests frailties too familiar to be dismissed as mere superficial delight.

After the First World War fashionable young women's dress deliberately minimized sexual characteristics and young men might wear make-up and androgynous or even deliberately female clothes. The bright young things of Evelyn Waugh's *Vile Bodies* (1930) insisted on a superficiality that one might think of as completely in

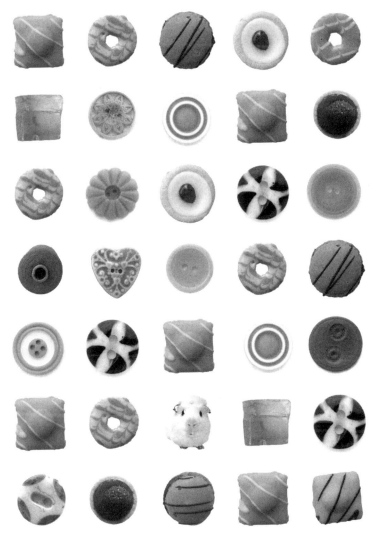

22. *All things Bright*, Kate Kessling, 2009. Pretty pastel colours: fancy mini cakes, iced biscuits, jelly cubes, a cute guinea pig and buttons.

keeping with the cute. Yet though they may have wanted to be thought young and careless, their style somehow betrays them. The evident effort involved in seeming carefree and spontaneous seems slightly at odds with cuteness. One might argue that, in the aftermath of the war, despite the cute behaviour of these young people, with deliberately high voices and practised gauche gestures, the harshness of that recent history lingers in the relative savagery of the charleston, and perhaps even the angular motifs and sometimes acid colours of their buttons. There is a tension between the apparent sweetness of the style and the guile required to achieve such a look.

It is during the thirties, when, despite the economic slump, or perhaps partly in response to it, mass-produced buttons often aimed to cheer and amuse. In *Modern Times* (1936), Charlie Chaplin is driven to a state of breakdown by the rigours of his assembly line factory job. Spanners in hand, he is drawn to the set of buttons on the rear of a young secretary, then chases a prim-looking middle-aged woman, wearing a pale dress with large dark buttons, accentuating her formidable bust. She screams in terror, realizing the crazed tramp-figure is determined to unscrew her buttons.

Plastics lent themselves to cute forms. At a time when many found themselves out of work, the short-lived sexual libertarianism disappeared, to be replaced by a return to darker clothing for the sober business of the economy. The effeminate beauty of male idols of the silver screen is replaced by men of a more rugged mien, conservative and adult in their style; their women are experienced sirens, wearing angular tailored suits themselves, buttoned up and able to give quite as good as they got.

The Art Deco movement invites a contrasting air of frivolity, seemingly at variance with the times. Its geometrical shapes and stylized natural forms, the use of vivid colours in geometric, linear designs, were a relief from a more general solemnity. On the one hand there are clean-lined modernist buttons, with a rather subdued earthy palette, but on the other there are buttons of sheer whimsy. I have a dress from this period, of a cheap, dark crêpe that appears to have been over-dyed, self-fabric shoulder-pads, grown limp with washing, but it is transformed even now by a row of exuberant Bakelite buttons in the shape of Scottie dogs with red spot bandanas. Such humorous shapes, sometimes called goofies or realistics, were popular into the 1940s and include animals, fish, birds, fairy-tale characters, fruit (*à la Carmen Miranda*), vegetables, almost every household knick-knack, from matchboxes to cutlery. Dogs are particularly prevalent, which seems to hark back to their popularity in the eighteenth century, but these dogs are comic and in no way intended to be naturalistic studies. The new plastics lent themselves to mass production, being quick and easy to pour into moulds and with integral non-fading colour. Many were produced of Walt Disney cartoon characters.

Elsa Schiaparelli was one of the first major designers to commission such novelty fastenings, using 'primitives' or buttons with, say, tribal African and Alaskan themes for her distinctive outfits. One of her jackets in the V&A archive, in bright pink, is part of her Circus Collection of 1938. It bears handmade cast metal buttons in the shape of diving girl acrobats. She also had buttons made in the shape of feathers, locks, paperweights, chains, animals and lollipops.

After the Second World War, Dior's New Look inspired a return to female glamour, and women seem older and more sophisticated – the hourglass shape of the new nipped-in waist, often with contrasting-coloured plain buttons as in the seminal Cecil Beaton photograph of cream jacket and full dark skirt, accentuating the adult female form. Gloves were often tightly buttoned to the wrist or worn in the evening, opera style. Men wore suits that accentuated breadth of shoulder, the double-breasted lounge suit buttons drawing attention to a powerful torso, or flattering a less fortunate one. The more Bohemian newly fashionable jeans look had metal rivets and fly buttons, and when worn tight, as by Elvis or James Dean, accentuate a more basic sexual divide (see Chapter 8).

We have seen how cuteness, buoyed up by commerce, creeps back into fashion, but sometimes a cute idea has stood the test of time. Contrary to some accounts, President Roosevelt was a keen hunter, but found it unsporting one day in 1902 to shoot a bear that had been tethered in order for him to achieve a kill. This incident was sentimentalized in the newspapers after a cartoon by Clifford Berryman represented the adult bear as a small cuddly cub, protected by a soft-hearted 'Teddy' Roosevelt. It is not certain who first produced a soft toy teddy, but the most successful brand came from Europe, in the form of Margarete Steiff's bear. In 1904 Franz Steiff, her nephew, invented the now legendary 'Button in the Ear' which was attached to the left ear, one of the first trademarks of the twentieth century. The button was made in nickel-plated iron, originally blank and later with the motif of an elephant stamped into it, the trunk forming the letter 'S'. However, by 1910 the word 'Steiff' was substituted, and can be dated by, for example, the earlier versions having the last 'F' of the logo stretching back under the lettering to the letter 'E'. By 1950 it is written in plain capitals with a simpler typeface.

The earliest bears with the blank logo are the most sought-after, a difficulty arising on account of later factory reject bears also being given blanks.

The concept of trademarks used for mass production to imbue conspicuous value, as against very similar articles that lack such a mark, is in principle cute and of enormous commercial potential. There had long been makers' names or trademarks on the back of buttons, often termed back-marks, but now such logos were placed for the observer to see clearly up front. We are so inured to trademarks today that it has become hard not to see them as intrinsic to an object rather than as extrinsic signage. A designer piece that has lost its label loses much of its market value – like an Old Master that has had its signature erased. In recent years even the most refined designers have taken to putting their marks on the outside of garments. Some have created textiles that have their logo forming a repeat pattern, or woven into the weave of linings, branded into the very fabric of clothes and declaring the 'slave-master' ownership. The clothes' value requires this out-and-out proof of lavish purchase. The name or sign becomes a fetish that magically invests the wearer with whatever reputation the designer enjoys.

Of course, there have long been club motifs that might be recognized by fellow members, but the trademark has a more universal appeal. The more it succeeds in convincing people to buy its products the more the logo is applied, so that the magic is felt not only of a designer's clothes say, but also that of almost any other object that bears the same brand. Part of the objective is to encourage people to aspire to the label that the conspicuous consumer displays. Sometimes a label can become so successful that it might be said to have vulgarized itself and thus to have failed to maintain its prestige. Yet such companies continue to sell well, and merely have to realign their manner of labelling in order to begin to adjust their image and so sell to the most affluent buyers again. The predator's claw, the *griffe*, can sink its talons into anything it likes: scent, T-shirts, even paper carriers bearing some fashionable monogram from top price designers, and sell for good money, even second-hand. Barbara Vinken describes:

> ... the all-powerful guarantee of a brand name, which has become a mythical signifier of fashion.

> (*Fashion Zeitgeist*, 2005, p. 85)

Those designers whose branded buttons are more discreet seem to have enjoyed a less steady reputation. However deft a subtle signal may be to those in the know, it cannot achieve the same level of visibility, and so appeals to less aspiring would-be buyers. Bill Gibb is a case in point, whose beautiful but understated bee button never achieved the secure position of more blatant designer buttons. It might be fanciful to link Gibb's choice to the favoured motif of Napoleon, that short-lived hero. The bee is a symbol of systematized industry, regeneration, wisdom and obedience and had a place in Egyptian, Roman and Christian thought. In contrast, the notoriety of the Duchess of Windsor brought the linked 'Cs' of the Coco Chanel brand to popular attention, a brand that still sells almost anything it chooses. The contemporary Turkish designer Isik Özgür uses buttons as a trademark aspect of her Ischiko clothes, and her website even has button images as navigation icons – but in the context of modern labelling her approach is subtle. Tucked away in the seams of her quirky pieces she conceals hidden buttons as trademark labels.

The Second World War utility scheme, instituted in 1941, was introduced to ensure consumer goods were produced to the highest possible standards given the limitations of the shortages and price constraints of war. Reginald Schipp designed the utility symbol, or 'the cheeses' as it came to be known, for civilian clothing. In *Vogue* magazine in 1942 the austerity specifications are spelt out, including the requirement for manufacturers to limit themselves to 'only so many buttons'.

Opportunities to trademark can be cleverly chosen and even beautiful, but they more often remain cute, in the sense that they are pretending to distinctive quality, when in fact the only thing that might distinguish a 'designer' plain T-shirt from a cheaper brand is arguably the authenticity of the mark alone. Some pretensions may be authentic, in that the trademark might indeed denote standards of design and quality. Nonetheless, they cannot in themselves make a piece of clothing more alluring, even if we have come to feel they do. We have sentimentalized the value of clothes.

In the past, couturier clothes did not always bear labels. According to Martyn Frith, tailors were the first to put trademarks on buttons. A tailor sold buttons claiming that they were the largest available; a rival tailor promptly had his larger buttons made emblazoned 'YOU LIAR', recalling Mary Shelley's present to Lord Byron (Chapter 8).

The great couturier houses of Europe have always valued the role of the button and thus their renowned *boutonnier* firms, such as Gossens. Rachel Kaplan describes visiting the atelier of Eduardo Braz, who worked with Christian Lacroix until his bankruptcy, and also Yves Saint Laurent, Christian Dior, Stéphanie Rolland, Alexis

Mabille and Alexander McQueen – the latter discusssing buttons for a future collection the day before his death.

Braz describes his role as making 'the "first line" – the one that the designer signs off on, and which is sold in the boutiques. It is made in France, not in China'. The process is painstaking and requires highly skilled craftsmanship. Designers might come to him with a theme 'such as Africa, Russia or something to do with folklore', for which he then makes a prototype button, which may have to be altered many times before satisfying the designer. In the lurch of Western society towards the impression of sumptuousness and the allure of fame, it is interesting that a great craftsman like Braz was most animated when describing his work for film companies, and in particular for the 1994 *La Reine Margot* and the fictive film opulence of sixteenth-century Paris.

It can be prohibitively expensive for craftspeople to adapt their work to a measure of mass production. The potter Lucie Rie was once asked by Wedgwood to produce a design for buttons, and she made prototypes in their familiar blue and white. However, the technical demands of her designs made it impractical for their production, given Wedgwood's knowledge of how much the public might be prepared to pay.

Buttons have become an easily available way of merchandising, or branding, goods, but the commonly recognizable monogram marks a sea change in what people want from aspirational clothes. No longer was it the flair and individuality of design and cut, but a proof that one was able to purchase a high-cost item. I do not mean to suggest that we might not delight in a designer's skill and imagination, but that most of us lack confidence in our powers of discrimination, and the trademark gives us Dutch courage.

However much cuteness has come to prevail, the twentieth century has a history no less dominated by conflict or the sorrows that sometimes punctuate even the most fortunate lives – and again, since its inception, the button has been indicative of both.

CHAPTER SIX

War and Grief

Giosue Orefice: Daddy, I cannot find any of the other kids, and a lady came telling me to take a shower.

Guido: Go take a shower!

Giosue: Buttons and soap.

Guido: What?

Giosue: They turn us into buttons and soap.

Guido: Who told you that?

Giosue: An old man was crying. He said they turn us into buttons and soap. ...They burn us all up in the ovens.

Guido: How ridiculous. They were teasing you!... Putting people in ovens causes too much smoke.

(Roberto Benigni, *La Vita è Bella*, 1997)

The button has been worn in the courts, clubs, ladies' salons and ballrooms of society at large. Yet there are darker haunts that we must enter now. If the button can breed status, then it has its place in the nefarious, the dangerous and the brutal.

Uniform buttons are a highly specialized area of study. Hardly any nation that has raised an army in modern times has failed to forge its own badges of honour and seniority. As uniforms began to be widely adopted in Europe and the United States, the separate regiments and affiliates could be designated by the button. These discriminations did as much for local spheres of influence as any hoped for national cohesion. In the First World War the British Army alone commissioned 367 types of buttons. Diana Epstein describes how any kind of button might be requisitioned within eight hours by front-line troops – that is, ordered, processed and arrived at the trenches within eight hours – so vital were they thought to be to morale. The British government reportedly spent over £600,000 per annum for the paste alone to polish these buttons. The act of keeping them clean, with special brass slides, or buttonsticks for keeping the polish from damaging the cloth beneath, remained an everyday duty during trench warfare. Perhaps its long-resented tedium might have been reassuring in those terrifying circumstances. Such buttons would have been attached to a garment with either an overlapping open ring of metal or a split pin, sometimes termed a cotter pin.

Each regiment and volunteer force could demand their own formal buttons. Button experts seek out evidence concerning those of long defunct brigades, some decimated by that war, or of corps that were planned but not formed, yet where sometimes distinguishing facets of uniform, including buttons, were produced. As late as 1970, for instance, an amalgamation of two regiments was planned as the Royal Regiment of Gloucestershire and Hampshire, and in preparation various items were produced such as stable belts and buttons, and which can now be viewed in the

Gloucester Rifles archive. The fact that the new joint regiment was never actually formed adds interest and value to such buttons. Naval, Air–Army Corps and later Air Force ranks all have their own minutely delineated categories of button. Buttons in military uniforms are less affected by fashion, yet they are often kept as memorials of war or keepsakes of fallen relatives after the uniform has been cut away. They also represent something stripped away from a dishonoured soldier at courts marshal.

Some of the most evocative buttons are arguably the least splendid. The masses of plastic standard issue shirt and trouser buttons, varying in shade of khaki for different climates and seasons, for desert colours or tropical jungle warfare, the white buttons of the polar expeditionary uniforms or dark brown from the shaggy-bear cold weather suits, all give evidence of their past. Two simple green buttons were used to attach a stretcher-bearer's armband as he struggled to transport the wounded back to relative safety. Many of such plain buttons were reused long after their original garments had been turned into cleaning rags. They are likely to be found at the bottom of any self-respecting button tin, scoring low in the game of sinkies but ideal for a stuffed toy's lost eye.

Then there are non-military uniform buttons, which again occupy a vast and diverse area of knowledge. The Russian court, for example, adorned its dress with thousands of gold and silver buttons. A relatively lowly nineteenth-century coachman's jacket, just part of what would have been everyday winter uniform, bears 99 plain gold buttons; buttons on such a servant's more formal livery would have been stamped with royal insignia.

In the annals of the uniform button one must also include the multitudes of less elevated monogrammed

servant and livery buttons; the buttons of nurses and aux-
iliaries and those of all the various categories of transport
from the merchant navies to buses, trains and trams; all
manner of clubs and organizations; the venery, including
those buttons intended for serving army officers, who,
when still on horseback, were assumed to hunt to hound.
The authority that a set of buttons might give a uniform has
become a conceit of the twentieth and twenty-first century
fashion world, when from the masculine-influenced Chanel
button to the 1980s power-dressing women in diluted gilt
mock-military buttons, to the New Romanticism of UK
bands such as Adam and the Ants and Spandau Ballet
using make-up and military buttoned uniform as a clash of
reference that spoke of androgyny.

In France the various buttons made before, during and
after the Revolution, which began in 1789, demonstrate
the shifting power of different allegiances: the trade went
on despite the Terror, but once established the new order
buttons might have been assumed to demonstrate a less-
ening of fashion-conscious display; yet the button capital
of the world continued to produce a sophisticated range.
Such was the pace of political change that buttons were
made to support a revolutionary figure, then quickly
supplanted as the tide changed. Buttons were made in
England to support martyred aristocrats. In Paris, early
on in the Revolution some were worn, at considerable risk,
in support of prisoners in the Bastille, emblazoned: 'Potius
more quam foedari' ('Better to die than to live without
honour'). Others espoused the Revolution by wearing buttons that ridiculed the excesses of the aristocracy. Despite
such harrowing political times, French politically inspired
buttons continued to be made using fashionable materials
and techniques, including jasperware, tombac, painting in

oil and gouache and engravings, while Hughes and Lester (1981) mention there being delicate wax models mounted under glass of political events.

Revolutionary buttons might declare a belief in change as in 'Vivre libre ou mourir!' ('Live free or die!') with fleur-de-lys as emblems of the French monarchy; or support the idea of a less despotic monarchy, 'La liberté est ma gloire' ('Liberty is my glory'). Cartoon buttons on paper under glass show scenes of the military, clergy and peasants supporting the intolerable burden of the king, or are represented by the symbols of sword, crosier and scythe. In the post-revolutionary period classical imagery was adopted to celebrate the new regime, with the oak wreath of victory and new-won authority perhaps combined with the Phrygian or liberty cap image, which may have been borrowed from American revolutionary wear (and later by Disney's seven dwarfs). Buttons were claimed to be fashioned from cannon taken from the Bastille after its destruction by the Parisian mob in 1789, one such memorializing the guillotined monarch, 'Au bon roi Louis XVI'.

In *About Buttons* Peggy Ann Osborne describes a period of intense sentimentalizing of the executed royal couple that led to a fashion for commemorative items, including portrait buttons, images of the monarchy, the Dauphin and notable aristocrats. Many apparently revolutionary buttons were in fact made for the centenary or later. The *jeunesse dorée* (golden youth), a counter-revolutionary group that held sway in 1794–5, inspired a fashionable genre of buttons a century later. Copper-rimmed watercolour paintings under glass declaiming 'Je terrasse les aristocrates' (I crush the aristocrats) are probably twentieth-century as their glass is flat rather than slightly convex, as it would have been in the eighteenth.

George III's head appeared on patriotic buttons in Britain, and images of Uncle Sam on American buttons, looking weary during the Spanish-American war of 1898. Political figures might be represented both to support a cause and sometimes to undermine one, such as the images of a slow-witted, plump possum in an anti-President Taft campaign. A possum feast was widely reported as having been enjoyed by Taft, after which possums were frequently sent as presents to the President, causing him to mildly remark that he did not quite 'hanker for it'. Nonetheless, possums continued to arrive for the portly head of state. The stars and stripes flag and the image of the spread eagle were popular among a new nation keen to stamp its identity on the world and are to be found on many sets of campaign buttons and on the new button-badges (see Chapter 10).

The first political buttons in the USA are probably those celebrating the inauguration of George Washington, which declared 'Long Live the President'. The new ferrotypes and tintype photographic buttons were rapidly adopted along with the new button-badge (see Chapter 10). In Britain patriotism tended to be expressed through the crown emblem.

During the Victorian period the image of the Queen, and to a lesser extent Prince Albert and her extended family, was worn by a large swathe of society, incorporating the new photographic techniques in ferrotype and tintype images. Cheaply made sets were also made to commemorate popular events such as Admiral Peary's expedition to the North Pole in 1909 and the erection of monuments like the Eiffel Tower in 1889.

Asylums and orphanages often had their own buttons made. Charles Dickens's *Oliver Twist* (1838) was based in part on the Foundling Hospital, built by Thomas Coram in London. This was one of the first such institutions, from as

early as 1741 taking in the babies and young children often
of destitute or desperate mothers. In line with their likely
future occupations, the girls' uniforms resembled those of
domestic servants; the boys were smarter and military in
style, and their red waistcoats bore brass buttons emblazoned with a Lamb Argent, from a design by William
Hogarth. This heraldic lamb is depicted with a sprig of
thyme in its mouth, suggesting, it is said, both elegance
and prowess, and perhaps more appropriately here it is
one of the herbs on which Mary, the mother of Jesus, is
said to have lain in the stable at Bethlehem, and so involves
a sense of courage in adversity. Moreover, the newborn
lamb suggests something full of life but vulnerable and
perhaps too meek for its survival.

For the Hospital to play the shepherd, it insisted on
severing contact between the children and their relatives.
Keepsakes were kept safe and carefully documented, but
in cruel irony, for fear of betraying the anonymity of the
parent, such mementos were never passed on to their offspring. The reasons for people giving up their children
sprung from poverty and various forms of necessity. From
the petitions that beg for admittance, it is evident that the
Hospital was thought of as a refuge of sorts, often a last
safe resort. Poor women had to prove their own good character in order for their children to be admitted.

In the gardens close by the Foundling Museum in
2009, Derek Wedgwood, describing himself as the oldest
Foundling Hospital committee member, explained that like
many through the years he had been a 'first born bastard'.
Illegitimate babies were joined by orphans of soldiers and
sailors; one letter from a father describes 'having a male
negro infant whom he is utterly unable to support and
maintain'; sometimes the infants were the result of rape.

One letter of petition, perhaps written by a literate friend
or one of those who would rent themselves out for this
purpose, reads as follows:

Dear Sir,

> I am the unfortunate woman that now lies under sen-
> tence of death at Newgatt (gaol). I had a child put in
> here when I was sent here his name is James Larney
> and this is John Larney... let them know one another,
> for dear sir I hear you are a very good gentleman and
> God Blessing be with you and they for ever.

Sir I am your humbled

Servant Margaret Larney

This woman's need to persuade, when she has so little
means to do so, is palpable. One does not know whether
her two sons were allowed to know each other as brothers,
for it is likely that their names would have been changed,
again for the sake of anonymity, and particularly with a
mother of such sad reputation.

The 'very good gentleman' was Captain Thomas Coram,
and his picture by Hogarth (1740), now hangs in the gallery
of the Foundling Museum. Unlike the other more formal
portraiture, he is wig-less, sitting comfortably, informally,
with a weather-worn kindly face, wearing still his red naval
brass-buttoned coat unbuttoned, his jacket beneath with
the buttons coming undone over his belly. In contrast, the
architect of the building, Theodore Jacobsen, is portrayed
in elegant classical pose leaning on a plinth, the buttons on
his cream satin, fashionably long waistcoat are embroidered
in red silk, his crimson velvet jacket has a gold taffeta lining
and silk velvet passementerie buttons (Hudson, 1746). The

Hospital became a fashionable place for the wealthy to visit, to view the first permanent exhibition space for British artists, to hear music played and, rather as at Bedlam, to enjoy the sight of the inmates. Captain Coram, after 17 years waiting for permission to set up the Foundling Hospital, must have considered them welcome enough, to secure the charitable donations on which he relied.

Among the many small keepsakes displayed in the Museum, among the thimbles, coins, a rusted padlock, a single hairpin, a key, some small pieces of intricate embroidery, there lies a single button, with what appears to be initials or even a rebus clue: Cm Gas. On occasion a paired item, a key to fit a keepsake lock, the missing half of a split coin or a matching button might be cherished by a relative in the hope of one day being reunited with their child. Perhaps a mother thought that button might bring her child one day to know its father, or perhaps it was simply the only thing she had of value. Was it her own family seal, or that of the father who had abandoned her? Perhaps it was just something found in the street, but nevertheless a token in trust for the child she could not keep.

The keepsake button recalls the sense of special value inherent in the collections of *Kindertransport* clothing of the Second World War. *Kindertransport* was the name given to the evacuation to the UK of nearly 10,000, mainly Jewish, children from Nazi Germany, Austria and Czechoslovakia just prior to the outbreak of the war. These children's and dolls' clothes they brought with them were nearly all homemade, often knitted and many kept as a memento of the care of the parents they had had to leave behind, with buttons on small cardigans and on the shoulders of jerseys, delicately smocked dresses with tiny mother-of-pearl buttons and calf leather buttoned baby shoes, now stiff with age.

Germany's two periods of heightened nationalism meant that emblems such as the crowned eagle were popular, and in the late 1930s the swastika button was produced for Nazi Party members. Victor Houart makes the point that the swastika was not used on buttons for the armed forces of the Third Reich.

The Royal British Legion memorial poppy buttonhole bears its own central black button, representing its motto, 'Remember the dead; do not forget the living'. Other nations, including Australia, Canada and New Zealand, have their own version, to commemorate all conflicts and life lost since the Armistice of 1918. The poppy symbolizes both sleep (as a source of opium) and death (its colour suggesting blood). In classical literature the colour of the poppy was associated with eternal life and thus the dead were brought offerings of poppies. The poppy of the buttonhole is the common field *Papaver rhoeas*, rather than the opium poppy, and can be found growing wild about the mud-filled trenches of northern France and later amongst the war graves there, as if to represent the fallen bloodied soldiers:

In Flanders fields the poppies blow
Between the crosses, row on row...

(John McCrae, 'In Flanders Fields', 1915)

It is claimed that the poppies grew in particular abundance during that war, possibly because the obliteration of crops and meadowland allowed the quick-growing weed to prosper. In 1933 the UK Women's Cooperative Guild produced a white poppy with a central white metal button incised with the word 'peace', which came to be adopted by various anti-war movements. It was claimed to be 'a symbol of grief for all people of all nationalities, armed forces and civilians alike'. Its association with conscientious objectors meant that it was often treated with antipathy, its wreathes trampled on and removed from the Cenotaph monument in London. During the 1980s Margaret Thatcher, the then British prime minister, said that she held it in 'deep distaste'. However, more recently, after the Twin Towers destruction of 9/11, white poppies were adopted to represent a call for peace.

Members of the Suffragette movement wore many varieties of button, often enamelled, to advertise their allegiance to the cause, usually bearing their colours of purple, green and white. Purple was to stand for the royal blood that coursed through the veins of the plucky suffragette, white standing for moral purity and green for the colour of spring and thus new life and hope for the future. Sometimes the purple was expressed in the form of a violet, which, as Jan Farrow explains, may have been so that the green, white and violet suggest the acronym GWV, as in 'Give Women the Vote' (Farrow, 2009, p. 19). Virginia Woolf reflects the colour in *The Waves*, referring to 'purple buttons and white foam'. She also, in contrast, suggests young women during the First World War running after men in uniform, attracted by their 'gilt buttons and braid'.

Military lapel buttons (not strictly buttons) were developed during the First World War. They were worn by the families of British fighting men – my grandmother wore a Royal Air Force lapel button in memory of a son until her own death in the early 1970s. Soldiers might wear them because uniforms were in short supply and thus the lapel button, particularly for the Volunteer Training Corps, the National Reserve and the Veteran Reserve, distinguished them from civilians who were not prepared to fight – and thus they may have avoided the risk of being thought a coward.

The danger in reviewing the past through the button is that it seems to cast a carefree jolliness on proceedings. One imagines the shiny brass buttons of an eighteenth-century red-coated uniform, or the swagger of young squaddies on parade in full dress gear, and one is perhaps reminded of tin soldiers, puppet men. Their purpose seems as innocuous as John Roberts's *War of the Buttons* (1994), where children from rival Irish villages cut off the buttons of the other side, and a hailstorm of buttons ensues. This film, and its French precursor directed by Yves Robert (1962), is based on a children's book by Louis Pergaud, and the clash between the notion of war and that of buttons is mirrored in the light-hearted irony of the title. The sentimentalizing effect of the presence of the word 'button' has perhaps tended to make their conjunction infantilizing and potentially comic.

These fictions were inspired by real events. In the seventeenth century a war of sorts had broken out between the button makers and tailors of France in what was called 'la Guerre des Boutons'. The button makers objected to the tailors' practice of making their own fabric buttons themselves, which made the specialists redundant. There were skirmishes and some blood was lost. Eventually the government passed a law to prohibit tailor-made buttons, fining them for thread and fabric button production, but still the button makers were not satisfied. However, since poorer people had long been making basic fabric buttons for their own needs, the button makers were unlikely to succeed in the long run, and the embargo was effectively broken. At any rate, Germany, Italy and Britain were fast developing their own button production, and the era of French dominance was coming to an end.

The poet Carl Sandburg captures the idea of war teetering between comedy and tragedy in his poem 'Buttons' (1905), where the board game of war is represented by a map plotting the progress of the warring armies with jolly coloured buttons:

> ... Who would guess what it cost to move two buttons one inch on the war map here in front of the newspaper office where the freckle-faced young man is laughing to us?

(Carl Sandburg, *Chicago Poems*, 1916)

The 'what it cost', the actual gamble with vast numbers of human lives, connects with the laughing man, his freckles betraying his proximity to childhood, and the light touch the poet employs implies both silly game and young fodder. However, our knowledge of Second World War concentration camps has brought this 'comedy' full circle. The Nazi organizational abilities that efficiently systematized the collection of clothing from concentration camp arrivals act as a grim alternative version of the button collectors' practice, recalling young Giosue's fear of being made into 'buttons and soap' at the beginning of the chapter. Many of the same aesthetic and organizational satisfactions seem to apply. It is rather like an exaggerated version of a current distaste for the idea of Victorian birds' eggs collections: despite a degree of moral reticence one may be impressed by the sheer scope and care taken. This curious ambiguity has fostered artwork, playing on this conflict of responses (see Chapter 9).

The Jewish Federation of Peoria, Illinois, set up a *Holocaust Memorial Button Project* in 2001 (peoriaholocaust-memorial.org). With the aim of showing the history of the

Nazi Holocaust in a tactile, comprehensible way, the buttons are of all shapes, sizes and qualities. Some 11 million buttons were collected to represent the 6 million Jews and 5 million 'enemies of the state' civilians killed by the Nazis. Those setting up the memorial felt that buttons were apt because of the way they both hold things together and yet can be easily undone: this collection was to stand for the strength and fragility of family and community. More concretely, they were memorials to the piles of clothing left at the gates of concentration camps, ghettos and slave camps, as easily disregarded as the suddenly 'disappeared', yet as enduring as the few survivors. The memorial itself was designed as 18 glass towers, in the shape of the Star of David, a number symbolizing the Hebrew *chai*, meaning 'life'. Two rows were to suggest the camp selection process of separating out those who would be allowed to live from those who would die, and five triangular shapes stood for non-Jews such as gypsies, homosexuals and the handicapped.

The Peoria Memorial must surely have influenced a community project in England, designed by Antonia Stowe, which was also intended to include the struggles of more recent refugees and asylum seekers: *6 Million +*, to mark Holocaust Memorial Day in January 2006 (BBC Bradford and West Yorkshire, 11 November 2005). Secondary school pupils across Kirklees were encouraged to collect buttons. The project leader, Kim Strickson, had at first considered paperclips instead, having heard of an American school that had collected them in memory of the Norwegian underground who had worn them on their lapels to show resistance to Nazi occupation. She wanted to find something readily available to the children that was equally resonant, and so the button, reminiscent of clothes taken from victims in the camps, seemed suitable. She has commented that buttons remained after clothing had disintegrated. Contributions were also accepted from the public, including one older woman, who gave a bag of 41 buttons to represent the 41 members of her family who had died in the Holocaust.

The installation has six transparent columns with buttons spilling out onto the floor below, suggesting that though 6 million may be the familiar figure, the full number of deaths is greater, impossible to calculate exactly, not to mention all the genocides that have taken place before and since that war. The children involved in the project were encouraged to imaginatively experience the vast numbers involved. The humdrum business of finding and bringing to the installation the diverse buttons they were able to acquire helped them appreciate that such bleak statistics are made up of separate individuals.

French artist Christian Boltanski, though alive to the horror of the Holocaust, allows an uncertainty regarding meaning and therefore allows more freedom for our response. He galvanizes a sense of collective memory in work that seems haunted by violence and a sense of loss, using photographs of schoolchildren in the 1930s (*Francois C*, 1971), piles of clothing and other objects belonging to the dead. His *Vitrine of Reference* (1971) consists of a box of photographs, hair, fabric, paper and earth – bringing to mind the specimen-like work of Joseph Beuys. Art appears to be taking up a scientific role, reminiscent of Damien Hirst's *Hymn* (1999), which is an enlargement of an anatomical model belonging to his son, or his pills in a cabinet, *Lullaby Spring*, 2007. We as viewer may ask what impression such specimens are intended to make on us. An artist presents us with a selection, an arrangement of found objects, and we may make connections to our own or learnt experience, but the space Beuys, Boltanski and Hirst leave allows us to make a response our own. I may want to feel when I view, say, a button placed next to some false teeth that this conjunction demands a response, and yet something in that manner of presentation inhibits me. I read that the artist has personal experience of the death camps, or of some more recent outrage, and I find I am moved. Even a button from one's button tin can feel redolent of its past, and it may remind one of horror, cruelty and despair as much as any more cosy sentiment.

Charles Ledray takes a possibly more oblique approach in his work *Mens Suits*, and this uncertainty of demand allows us as audience to come to any tentative conclusions more gradually, and its impact is all the greater. He is determined to deflect any attempt to explain, or explain away his work, and though it is hard to avoid trying to work out reasons for the understated impression his work tends to make, looking through his archive he seems to have been claimed by many different interest groups. I am mentioning him here, for example, as evidence of buttons in art in relation to war and the Holocaust in particular, and although that may have relevance, his purpose still seems mysteriously just out of reach. Regarding *Mens Suits*, one might just as well argue for a pre-eminent theme of consumerism, or perhaps a more pervasive sense of our mortal fragility. He has carved buttons himself, he says, out of human bone. We read this bald fact in his press release of 7 August 2009, and I think he must intend that we attempt to understand why.

Mens Suits was commissioned by London-based Artangel, and was housed in a disused fire station exhibition space in 2009. There is, by the way, no apostrophe in the title, which might make one feel immediately irritated or baffled. Is it just a silly mistake or a comment on the sorts of mistakes that are made? Does he mean that nothing is possessed here and that the clothes are abandoned, or does he just want to unsettle us with the question of what is grammatically appropriate? The visitor enters a rather murky warehouse space, which seems to be divided into three rooms. There is very little natural light and as I adjust my vision there is a feeling of deflation. I notice with disappointment that I am, Alice-like, plainly too large. These rooms are intended for smaller people and I will have to bend down awkwardly in order to see into them properly. The clothes don't look cute. Nor do they look as if they were for children exactly. I had read about the exhibition and knew to expect something in miniature, but this is not the miniature I had expected. It is too big for that: it is neither one thing nor the other. An assistant informs me that Charles Ledray is tall and broad, so this oddness of scale had to be deliberate. But why? And why is the scale so disconcerting?

The three 'rooms' are suggested by four separate 'ceilings', suspended from the warehouse roof and bearing some dimly lit panels. Above these ceilings, because of the reduced scale, one could make out motes of dust apparently brought over with the artist from America, and what light there was seemed also to dance with dust. Stooping down to see into each room, one seemed to have arrived in the offices of a charity shop. In one of these the clothes have just arrived, dumped in rubbish sacks and spilling out of laundry bags onto the patched lino-tiled floor, some stacked on pallets to keep them from getting damp, perhaps. The donations were in the process of being sorted, and in another room an ironing board stands ready, a headless dummy the only 'human' figure present. The remaining space is the shop itself, clothes now ordered and tidy, but an air of despair remains.

Despite this sombre mood one is drawn into inspecting the clothes: they are child-sized. It took Ledray three years to make every item, every prop, garment and button, and whereas at first they seem random, they capture an artist's feel for discordant colour and pattern combination (*Evening Standard*, 16 July 2009). There are limp, worn-out shirts, dreary check sports' jackets, the dismal fans of ties – all made to scale, yet sometimes uneasily so, the fabric designs seeming not quite right in proportion. The artist also constructed the scaled-down rails and hangers, one declaring in discordant jollity 'We Love Our Customers'.

Initially it was disappointing to find that there was very little variation in the buttons: plain, round and pale or dark, and all of a similar size. Often they seemed either slightly too large or small for the scale of the garment. I had half expected there to be some message to be deciphered from the choices Ledray made. Of course, there was, only I had been unable to anticipate its mysterious complexity. It has been remarked that the handsewn clothes are perfectly scaled-down versions of reality, but I think this is not quite so. They are disturbingly aberrant, and it is only in the minutiae of detail that this becomes clear. Peter Campbell, in the *London Review of Books* (6 August 2009), describes this as the rub between 'what is and is not exactly to scale hold(ing) your attention' and draws a comparison with Jenny Wren, the dolls' dressmaker in Dickens's *Our Mutual Friend*.

Ledray insists that he wants his work to be photographed in such a way that the reduced scale is not obvious, so that perhaps what Ossian Ward calls 'that zone of *unheimlich* uncanniness' (*Time Out*, 23 July 2009) can be inferred even by someone not present at the installation. You must judge for yourself whether the image printed in the colour section draws you into a thrift shop 'reality' or whether the incongruities ask you to question the artist's intent. Ledray has said of an earlier work that 'there are no ordinary objects. All things have potential'. Is his claim that they are human bone buttons an elegant mischief, or does he intend this information to make us take the clothes more seriously, and encourage us to see the installation as a sort of graveyard of past lives?

An earlier work, *Buttons* (2000–2), displays 130 buttons in various shapes and sizes. They, too, are said to be of human bone, and their colour ranges from whites and ivory to greyish pink. Another piece of 1999, *Door*, fashions a tiny door, again purportedly of human bone, which he claims to have purchased from a mail-order catalogue. His craftsmanship evokes the efforts of the Jewish inhabitants of Łódź Ghetto in Poland during the Nazi occupation. Despite enormous hardship, food shortages and imminent deportation to the death camps, a skilled workforce became a major producer of buttons for the Reich. A set of trouser buttons in the Imperial War Museum might almost be the work of Ledray. If the clothes in *Mens Suits* seem lifeless yet differentiated, the parallel with the piles of documented death camp clothing and what they represent is only too apparent.

My father was posted behind the lines in Japanese occupied Burma, and later recalled a senior officer who gloried in a swagger stick and buttons fashioned, the man had claimed, from enemy thighbone. This making of the essence of the enemy into a familiar everyday object is akin to the headshrinker gaining status by such possession.

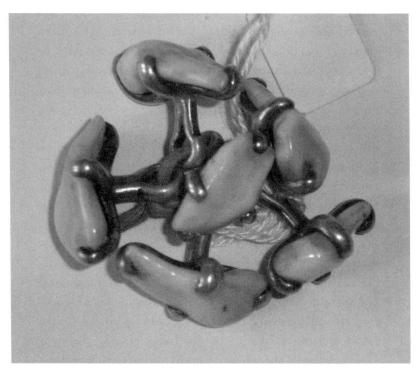

23. Dog's teeth with silver button backs, which are more likely fond mementos of a beloved companion, worn in somewhat macabre respect.

From Changi Prison in Singapore, where civilian internees were held by the Japanese occupying army, a pair of underpants of one Vincent Beck survives. They are handmade, with buttons up one hip, ironically inscribed, 'our own make'.

As well as the poison-filled buttons carried by commando troops and issued on spying missions in case of torture, or those designed to puncture skin with a hidden spike and so surreptitiously murder in seventeenth-century Italy, some forces wore buttons that concealed escape compasses, for navigation if lost behind enemy lines. Under the auspices of M19, over 2 million compasses of various designs were issued during the Second World War. Donald Nicholson, now 87, should have been flying in a Lancaster with his crew when they were shot down over Germany on their sixth raid together. He had suddenly been taken ill and so escaped the fate of the three who managed to bail out and were taken prisoner, and of the remaining four who were killed, including his best friend. In 2009 Nicholson describes how he still treasured his friend's secret compass, which had been left behind in his locker (Katy Simpson, *Evening Chronicle*, 19 August 2009).

Like some of the poison examples, the compass buttons have the appearance of standard brass buttons, though the Royal Air Force ones unscrew to the left, the Royal Navy to the right, in an attempt to confuse the enemy, it is said. One cannot help feeling that if the enemy had come to be searching for your trick button, the game might already be up and thus the question as to which way it undid might become obsolete. Another type used had a pressure fit closure, rather like contemporary child-safe medicine bottle tops. Such hidden compasses were intended to be part of an emergency kit, hidden amongst various places, in cap buttons, collar studs and trouser buttons.

Smugglers have long carried contraband hidden in buttons. In the 1942 film *Blue, White and Perfect*, a Nazi smuggling ring steals industrial diamonds from an Allied aircraft plant, destined we are told for Hitler's dress buttons. Many of the concealed functions hidden in James Bond's fictional buttons, designed by the ingenious Q, have been proven to have some foundation in fact. The more such technology is developed and made available to us, with hidden computer chips providing two-way radio transmission or acting as detonating triggers for explosive devices, the less fantastic Bond's adventures seem. More prosaically, one Sony Dong, travelling from Vietnam to the United States in 2009, was caught by airport inspectors smuggling 13 rare songbirds strapped to his legs with the aid of small fabric pouches attached to buttons sewn onto his socks. He was given away when droppings and feathers were spotted on his ankles (National Geographic News, 6 May 2009).

In Second World War Britain, women and men unfit for combat were encouraged to join the Dig for Victory campaign. During the period from 1939 to 1943 allotments increased in number from 815,000 to 1,400,000. The campaign was publicized not just in order to supplement wartime rationing but as a way of promoting patriotism, and one among many means of showing you cared was to wear a dress of brightly coloured fabric, overprinted with vegetables and the Dig for Victory slogan, picked out on the self-covered buttons. Wartime shortages meant buttons were often used as a relatively inexpensive way of cheering up tired clothes, typified by the cheap and cheerful American Walt Disney plastics.

Towards the end of that war, American GIs still based in England were able to receive some university-level courses at Shrivenham, a former British Army training camp (Dickman, 1946). Over 300 mainly American university professors were employed to help the troops 'escape the khaki'. There were trips to Stratford-on-Avon for the theatre, practical training in farming techniques and notably two English girls were employed to assist the less academic in various ways from 'sewing on buttons to arranging a honeymoon'.

The aptly named death's-head button has been in existence since the seventeenth century. It cannot help but remind one now of the Death's Head insignia on the collar patch of Second World War death camp guards. However, it existed as an image long before, as did the swastika motif, which had sprung from ancient Hindu culture, and can be found on Indian silver buttons from the nineteenth century. The death's-head is a form of the Leek button, and it is built up on a wooden or perhaps horn base over which threads are tacked and then oversewn. Unlike the passementerie button, these are more lowly, with no silver or gold thread used. The death's-head thread is woven into an 'X' formation, forming four segments, suggesting the four humours of classical origins, those bodily fluids that were thought to determine our emotional and physical dispositions. The pattern is said to have got its name from the crossed thighbones of a skull and crossbones, that piratical symbol of danger and death.

In the peace between the two world wars, prohibition in the United States fostered gangster culture, the lower ranks of which were known, particularly amongst the Mafia, as button men, a term that has continued to be used. Such men do the dirty work for their bosses: they are employed to push a button on someone. In Joseph Wambaugh's 1981 novel *The Glitter Dome*, one character opposed to gang warfare claims, 'all we're trying to do is stop the button men from hitting the mattresses'.

There are many anecdotal accounts of buttons saving lives from sword or bullet. *The New York Times* reports a farmer's life being saved when an assailant shot him from behind:

> The bullet went through a heavy fur coat he wore and drove the suspender button into the small of his back, inflicting only a superficial wound.
>
> (*New York Times*, 12 December 1912)

More ignominiously, buttons might be the only thing one had of value left to steal when down and out of luck. In an episode of CBS's *Have Gun – Will Travel*, Manfred Holt is under arrest and anticipates the worst:

> To be hung at a country fair, while they hawk the buttons off your shirt. Thanks.
>
> (*The Outlaw*, 1957, 1. 2)

There are, of course, examples of people prepared to steal buttons, such as Felicidad Noriega, the wife of the ex-President of Panama, who accepted a plea bargain to stay out of prison after being caught cutting the buttons off designer garments in Miami in 1992. They must have been fine buttons to risk such disgrace and to warrant a fine of $1,321 plus a community service order (*LA Times*, 25 March 1992). One might think one could get away with button theft. More poignantly, Mary Sortile, the owner of Exclusive Buttons in El Cerrito, had a button belonging to her husband that had decades before been discovered by some railway tracks, stolen only a few weeks after his death. It was a fifteenth-century button adorned with hand-painted butterflies, which had been turned into a brooch. 'I wouldn't have minded if [the thief] took anything else in the store,' she said (N'Jeri Eaton, *El Cerrito Focus*, 12 November 2008).

If buttons have been significant in terms of violence and war, how well do they serve as *memento mori*? We think of such tokens as being sentimental reminders of lost loved ones, yet in the past they were intended to be a reminder to oneself of the imminence of death, meaning, literally, 'remember you shall die'. Thus images of clasped hands, skeletons or skulls are a direct warning, in case we forget this unavoidable truth.

The many early hair buttons are thus a moral warning and act as a reminder to the individual, rather than being a token of regret or lingering affection for the dead. Hair was imported into Britain as early as the late seventeenth century. Eighteenth-century hair buttons fall into two main categories, woven and painted. The former were known as basket weave or basket buttons. Hair was braided and held in place under glass, usually with a copper rim. The painted variety was rarer, a paint being made from a mixture of ground hair and sepia tint, which was then painted onto ivory or bone in microscopic detail. Different shades were achieved through using different coloured hair, and sometimes strands of hair were attached whole, to depict lines of a bridge say, small sections for the silver crests of waves, or grasses in a landscape. The way light reflects on natural hair allows the artist the possibility of a subtle interplay of light and shade. Not all this hair button work seems to have been for *memento mori,* since the subject matter can be light-hearted and even irreverent with bucolic neoclassical scenes of frolicking shepherds and shepherdesses, pleasure-boating and rural fishing.

The quantity of hair required for these buttons was enormous, not to mention that used for hairpieces and jewellery. One might lose a husband and then walk around in cheery buttons fashioned from his sadly departed handlebar moustache. France alone provided 100 tons a year towards the latter half of the nineteenth century. The wearing of hair-based sentimental products became a popular fad, and it is likely that Prince Albert's death in 1861 also had a major effect on how mourning came to be seen – as a fashionable state requiring fashionable adornment.

Other buttons such as tintypes or ferrotypes satisfied the taste for the sentimental. After the development of celluloid these allowed the use of photographic images: it became possible for a soldier to carry an image of a film star, girlfriend or wife to the trenches, or vouchsafe his own image. In some contrast, the effect of the extraordinary single human eye buttons in Diana Epstein and Millicent Safro's collection, where the eye of the deceased stares coolly back, seem astonishingly serious. They were made on a base of ivory, enamel or paper, often by skilled miniaturists. Separated from their facial context the eyes seem eerily inscrutable.

The artist Kate Kessling, on learning about these eye buttons, gave the subject her own witty attention. Her 15-year-old daughter Mirren had broken up with a boyfriend: having taken this to heart, and unable perhaps to believe that the world could be so unkind, she was awash with tears. Fortunately for this project, Kessling took digital

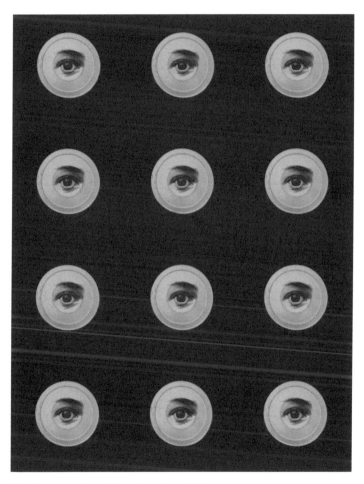

24. *Mourning Eye*, Kate Kessling, 2009.

25. Jet mourning buttons and a photograph of them being worn, late nineteenth century. The 'natural' setting suggests that, despite the formal attire, grief is a wild and uncontrollable emotion.

photographs of her daughter's crying eyes and produced her own take on mourning buttons, a contemporary *memento mori* for lost young love.

Queen Victoria's refusal to come out of mourning for the remaining years of her life had an influence across the then British Empire. Black remained the predominant fashion colour for over two decades, and it was not uncommon for a woman once widowed to follow Victoria's path and wear black for the rest of her life. Commercially speaking, this was a boon for the Yorkshire fishing village of Whitby, where jet, a form of prehistoric driftwood, was to be found washed up on its shores. Jet is an extremely hard variety of coal that can be polished and made into jewellery, and it was used in some of the finest examples of handmade buttons. It was scarce enough to be expensive, and since it was also very fragile, black glass became a more affordable and practical substitute. Black glass was manufactured in Italy, Bohemia and Austria and later in North America. True jet, unlike glass, is warm to the touch and light in weight. Any old family photograph album will furnish one with relatives in black, and if they were of sufficient affluence, a glint of light may suggest their glass or possibly jet buttons. The effect of this fashion was pervasive and still invades our attitude to death and dying.

Another popular emblem of grief and mourning, even among the poor, was a silk flower, usually white or grey in colour, with a black button at its centre – a precursor of the British Legion poppy emblem. These might then be transferred in due course to adorn a photograph of the departed. In similar fashion other charities have adopted buttonholes as a way of advertising their cause, and a flower is more often used to suggest the idea of both fragility and youth, as for example with the daffodil adopted by Marie Curie Cancer Care: a poppy, like the wild dog rose of Alexandra Rose Day, shrivels and dies quickly if it is picked; a daffodil is something associated with early spring, youth and hope.

Buttons have been used as a form of currency, as in silver buttons in Mexico during the eighteenth century, often in the form of facsimiles of Spanish coinage or miniatures of the Spanish royal crest. Genuine Spanish coins were sometimes converted into buttons with the addition of a simple looped wire shank. These might then be further adapted and used as cuff links, while still amenable to conversion into ready money, and were used in many countries as such.

The American textile artist Jane Burch Cochran makes fabric quilts closely trapped with all manner of buttons. Her gathered, or 'yo-yo' flowers, are tied through several layers to the back of the quilt with buttons, which become their centres. In Mexico the official flower of the dead is the marigold, which Cochran represents with brilliant yellow yo-yos with button centres (see colour plate section). Cochran became interested in the Dia de los Muertos, or the Day of the Dead, after visiting the village of Patzucuaro in Mexico – she wanted:

> to capture some of the spirit of this magic event. The simple dirt graves are transformed with flowers (especially marigolds), candles, sugar skulls etc. for the holiday when the souls come back to visit their loved ones.

(www.janeburchcochran.com, 2010)

The vivid colour seems joyous and yet the buttons depict what is lost; Cochran also uses buttons for the eyes of the dead, lined up and staring blankly back.

I have suggested how the button has been used in relation to conflict and how it can act as a small reminder of past disappointments and loss, but in the sphere of religion and cultural distinction it has been equally influential.

CHAPTER SEVEN

Culture and Creed

The history of the button is bound up with European and North American culture, but there are exceptions. Not only did the rest of the world inspire and to a great extent produce the raw materials and necessary skills required, but there are also examples of the button independent of European influence, in diverse forms.

Much clothing tends to be wrapped or bound about the body and often secured with a form of fabric belt alone. Generally speaking, this style often falls under the catchall of the 'ethnic', but, in reality, where buttons have been required, they do seem to have been used. Of course, this is something of a chicken and egg argument. However, it is interesting to note that where buttons have been adopted, until relatively modern times they have been largely worn by men.

Although in ancient civilizations such as those of the American Indians, Incas and Egyptians people appear to have decorated their clothes with beads and stones, it is hard, as has been mentioned, to find evidence that they were used for fastening purposes. One of the problems in

26. European buttons decorate a black, scarlet and indigo embroidered ceremonial dress, early twentieth century, and as with many traditional costumes the buttons are purely decorative.

dating when and where buttons were used is not only that early garments are likely to have rotted away, but also that fabric buttons and any toggle and loop system would have met the same fate. Moreover, it is hard to decipher from illustrations that might decorate porcelain, say, whether there are buttons present. Certainly early Chinese robes usually carry five buttons, often in the familiar knotted fabric form, sometimes with the twisted loop catch and oval buttons known as mandarin frogs representing the five Confucian virtues of humanity, justice, order, prudence and rectitude. Toggle-like buttons were also used on outer overcoats and to fasten boots and bags.

In sixteenth-century Japan, a samurai warrior might wear over his armour a surcoat known as a *jinbaori* (Kite, 1998). Initially designed to protect the armour, these coats became an important symbol of samurai status. One such housed at the V&A in London is a splendid example in silk, richly embroidered with metal threads and decorated with peacock feathers. The back of the collar and long revers are covered in Chinese silk, as are the backs of the fastening tabs. Significantly, horn buttons fasten back the revers and would also have held the tab fastenings closed. The coat was first thought to be a theatrical costume for an angel, perhaps in a traditional Noh drama, but recently it was identified as an original samurai surcoat. It might well have been worn into battle as a symbol of the warrior's taste and prowess, the peacock feathers suggesting male beauty and arrogant display.

Kimonos do not have pockets, so traditionally small leather pouches, or *sagemono*, were hung from a sash belt, or *obi*, by silken cords. The small toggles used to fasten these pouches are the renowned *netsuke*, which literally means 'to attach the root'. Although early *netsuke* are quite simple, perhaps using a stone, shell or small gourd, gradually they developed into a sophisticated art form, employing many of the most gifted craftsmen (Zipser, 1996). The work is essentially sculpture in miniature and is made from all manner of natural materials such as wood, ivory and bone, walrus tusk and whale tooth, tortoiseshell, black coral, metal, ceramics, the sought-after fossilized wood *umoregi*, and even nuts and seed pods; nowadays the unwary may find themselves purchasing counterfeit plastic 'ancient' *netsuke* at inflated prices.

As the art developed one might argue that *netsuke* become less like a button in function and form, yet the slim *manju netsuke*, round and flat, does still resemble a button. In Japan a *manju* is a flattened rice cake, thus this part of a *netsuke* is associated with something fundamental and hon-oured within Japanese society. They can be made in solid ivory or wood, and sometimes they are finely carved and reticulated. This more elaborate type is known as a *ryusa netsuke*. The designs are influenced by Chinese mythol-ogy as much as the fables and history of Japan. However, during the period when Japan became isolated from the rest of the world,[1] Japanese themes were predominant as a matter of political and ideological choice. The mode and manner of *netsuke* making training and practice became tightly regulated and of necessity closed to influence from abroad. Although in modern times standards have inevi-tably fallen, in order to satisfy the export demand of col-lectors, some contemporary *netsuke* continue to be made of high quality and are thought of as art in their own right, with new non-traditional designs such as computers and characters in modern-day dress. At the same time, some of the eighteenth-century *manju netsuke* can seem startlingly modern.

27. This flattened rice cake-like ivory *manju netsuke,* decorated with the carved figure of Princess Wakana, gaining spiritual powers from a spider spirit. By Reigyoku, Japan 1859–1900.

In some *netsuke* Japanese brass buttons, *kagagami-buta*, are used at the centre of an ivory body. They are in low relief, and embellished with gold, silver or other metals, and draw on the traditional craft skills of samurai sword makers. They depict natural objects, flora and fauna, and sometimes comic scenes from Chinese and Japanese folk tales. The extraordinary realistic detail of the Japanese subject matter is in some contrast to the European more impressionistic and generalized naturalism of, say, early French eighteenth-century examples. Imports from China and Japan had a lasting effect on European natural-ism, encouraging the notion of close observation and life drawing.

Satsuma ware buttons exported from Japan in the latter part of the nineteenth century seem to have been produced only for foreign markets, yet rely thematically on a distinc-tive style developed as early as the seventeenth century. Originally they were used for kimonos and kimono coats and were usually small in size, hallmarked on the back with a circle enclosing a cross with the maker's name beneath. Satsuma ware is made from earthenware or porcelain in an off-white or cream colour, and then finely overglazed. This thin translucent glaze is then deliberately overheated to achieve the typical cracked finish and achieves a warmth and richness, which is then, sometimes quite heavily, embellished with gilding. The traditional forms of blossom, chrysanthemums and the thousand cranes, often alluding to themes in haiku poems, along with the frogs, locusts, cicadas, men and women, geishas and peasant figures, some buttons with rounded crenellated edges, are in some contrast to those made after the Exposition Universelle in Paris in 1867. On the one hand, as they were increasingly made for export only, there is evidence of some Western techniques beginning to be used, but on the other, the painting becomes less finely detailed and the images less complex. In making buttons for the Europeans, perhaps the button makers' link with their cultural source began to be lost.

Many of what appear to be Japanese and Chinese buttons are in fact copies, sometimes simplified in design, often made in European factories, though in the Waddesdon collection there is a set of true Japanese cloisonné enamel designs with arches of cherry blossom set against a sky blue background. The sophisticated cloisonné technique involves wires being gently soldered to a metal base to create walls and hollows into which the coloured enamels are poured. Such buttons were increasingly popular in the early 1920s, in line with the vogue for things 'oriental'. There was also a tradition of fine ivory buttons, sometimes with inlaid designs, using semi-precious stones and mother-of-pearl. Sometimes the ivory is etched with delicately painted colour. These various examples from Japan all reflect its geographical isolation in terms of design and in the craft techniques that had thus had time to be perfected, unchallenged during that period by competitive forces.

In the second half of the nineteenth-century Navajo Indians, of the south-western part of North America, were encouraged to take up the art of the silversmith. Together with the Pueblo Peoples of the same region, and initially with the most primitive tools and improvised forges, they began to develop a distinctive style of jewellery, including the button (Anderson, 1955). They incorporated age-old tribal symbols, designs of shells, stars, Indian horses and snakes, using silver, copper, inlaid gemstones and beading.

Though the Navajo, in particular after the end of intern-ment in 1868, may have been pressed to take up the skill by colonizing authorities, they made it their distinctive own. It is likely that they already had some experience, as Major Henry Wallen, Commandant of Fort Sumner commented in 1864: 'Some of them are quite clever at silversmithing.' In 1853 the Indian Agent to the Navajo, Captain Henry Linn Dodge, brought blacksmith George Carter to Fort Defiance to teach ironwork. Moreover, Dodge's transla-tor happened also to be a skilful silversmith. The Indians began to utilize horse tackle or Spanish coins both to sell to order and to develop their own distinctive button designs. They might be given old silver teapots or candlesticks to melt down by their settler customers, but although it became prohibited, silver coins were still easier to use and thus more popular.

The first Navajo silversmith was Atsidi Sani, who died in 1918. Sani, also known as Old Smith and Herrero Delgado, was learning blacksmithing from as early as 1853 under the itinerant Mexican smith Nakai Tsosi, or Thin Mexican. His first student was Grey Moustache, his great-nephew, and he went on to introduce his craft to the Zuni, Hopi and Rio Grand Pueblos. The indigenous tribes had come into contact with the Spanish from as early as the late sixteenth century and so had some know-ledge of Spanish jewellery, and today some Navajo designs involve Moorish-inspired crescents and pomegranate blos-som. Sani's own sons became silversmiths: Little Smith, Red Smith, Big Black and Burnt Whiskers. His younger brother, Slender Maker of Silver, became one of the best silversmiths of his time. Indeed, Sani himself was so successful that from being only a very minor tribal head, by 1858 he had become a prominent chief. One might say that his skill as a silversmith, in part as a button maker, led to him being one of the chiefs to sign the treaty of 1868, to return the Navajo to their ancestral lands.

The earliest buttons made for the Native Indians' own use were fluted or domed, gradually becoming more elaborate, using turquoise and garnets in the main. In the late 1930s the Hopi developed their own style, using an overlay technique, cutting the designs in heavy gauge silver sheet, then soldering this to a solid silver base. Today artists like Ray Chrley work on modern Navajo designs, still grounded in the early Spanish influence, Navajo mythology, Hopi kachina symbols and clan motifs, including animals and insects such as spiders and scorpions. Chrley's ant buttons have backs inset with onyx, turquoise, coral and peridot.

In Pakistan, India and Bangladesh the idea of 'stitched' clothing has had an ambiguous connotation, both of progress and more negatively of imposed Western influence, yet early examples of collarless shirts and waistcoats (introduced by the Pathans of the North West Frontier Province) have self-covered buttons, sometimes elaborately embroidered and having very much the appearance of passementerie. This may have been the knock-on effect of Western-style military uniforms, and one might also argue that the influence of the seventeenth-century European aristocrat can in turn be traced in its general shape to the *salwar kameez*, itself an import from Turkey and Afghanistan. There are examples of maharajas' buttons from the early eighteenth century, richly embellished and made in similar designs to those of jewels like the *sarpech*, or turban ornaments, studded with rubies, diamonds, emeralds, sapphires and pearls, suggesting that they were quickly assimilated into native Indian workmanship. In the early twentieth century buttoned clothing came to be associated with Westernization, as in the revere-less, stand-up collared Nehru suit, as opposed to wrapped clothing like the sari and the dhoti, as adopted by Mahatma Gandhi.

Iceland's traditional dress for women includes decorative aprons that are held in place at the waistband by large buttons in sets of three. They are usually round or hemispherical, shallow and drum-shaped, and importantly wholly unique to Iceland. Some examples made out of sheet silver are hollow, and then gilded with a picture of the crucifixion or other, usually religious, images, sometimes surrounded by crowns and scrolls of imitation filigree. Those in the archive of the V&A have a medieval appearance, due to their elaborate border, but are thought to be eighteenth or nineteenth century. It is likely that Iceland's geographical isolation intensified and to some extent protected traditional design. At any rate, in Iceland, Lapland and other remote areas of north-west Europe, traditional jewellery has retained a medieval character that has been lost elsewhere, and these buttons continue to carry a weight of cultural and religious significance. It would seem likely, though I have not seen this point expressly made, that Alaskan walrus-ivory buttons were made for visitors, and seem to date from the mid-nineteenth century. Earlier examples are three-dimensional, depicting walruses, fish and seals and some in carved relief-work with their features picked out in pigment. In the early twentieth century the work becomes less fine and includes primitive etchings of Inuit in native costumes.

In Africa, apart from button-like adornments, on the whole buttons seem to have been produced for foreigners

28. Lapland and Iceland, so remote that though this exquisite
button is probably eighteenth or nineteenth century, it remains
medieval in style. Icelandic repoussé silver, gilded on the front.
1700–1850.

and export, usually in carved ebony, teak and ivory, sometimes inlaid with silver or bone. The fashion for the primitive in 1920s Europe and the interest of the art world in the African aesthetic, typified by sculptors like Constantin Brancusi and Jacob Epstein, also fuelled an appetite for African artefacts and design. Buttons produced were in the form of native heads or masks and of wild animals; such images were often invested with a spiritual significance by the craftsperson, but that was most likely to be lost in translation to the West and into the foreign button.

In Ethiopia in the 1970s, after the overthrow of Haili Selassie, the arts were severely disrupted and only works of political propaganda were permitted. When the Durg regime was overthrown, the artistic renaissance fostered work by artists such as Elias Simé, who makes collages with what is thrown away, such as bottle tops, tattered clothing and, needless to say, buttons (Latimer, 2009).

Korean fabric-covered buttons are part of traditional costume, or *hanbock*. These buttons, or *hoback*, are large, plain discs of amber, slightly tear-shaped, with the point of the tear sewn pointing upwards, and as with Chinese traditional buttons, closed with fabric loops. The use of the fossil amber is important, I was told, as it is held to symbolize the timelessness of such robes.

The Korean artist Ran Hwang uses buttons as an essential part of her armoury. The troubled history of Korea and Hwang's Buddhist convictions make her work seem at first strangely opaque. She makes three-dimensional collages, such as a number of shallow boxes filled with buttons that are then made visible through a cut-out silhouette, many in the shape of an urn, an object of significance as a container for the ashes of the dead. Her large-scale wall installations, all using buttons, pins and thread, often have a hovering figure of Buddha, usually off-centre. Yet when the image is present, and made out of buttons, the gap between the ordinary and a deity is curious: does she ennoble the commonplace or undercut the elevated? Images of Buddha are often used as a fashionable icon of Eastern connotation, so perhaps Hwang is asking us to review the familiar fashion and consider its true significance.

The artist describes a childhood steeped in Buddhist practice followed by a period when she was abruptly confronted by the West, when she moved to New York. She believes that 9/11 had a great influence upon her work and, most pertinently here, that event helps to explain the piles of loose buttons often found beneath her work. She was struck by images of people and detritus, or 'buttons and ash' as she describes it, falling from the Twin Towers. The larger works are formed by an unusual process of construction, hammering pins at differing angles and heights into a base board, and from these hang the buttons. She remarks that she finds this repetitive process therapeutic, describing it as a form of meditation, as if she wants her life as an artist to mirror the menial peasant work she had witnessed as a child:

> I injured my fingers many times in the process of hammering. As I hammer each pin, my past scar disappears and I fall into peaceful moment.

> (Personal communication, 23 October 2009)

Gradually, over time, buttons become dislodged and fall to the ground, recalling the falling debris Hwang had witnessed. Some of these images are made entirely using

29. Ran Hwang, *Empty Me*, detail, 2009. See colour plate section.

pearl white buttons and take on an eerie, ghostly quality, like her great white birds for example, their feathers seeming to fall to the ground in flight, and they have a deliberately unfinished appearance. A vast eagle she completed within a disused prison in Korea suggests the idea that such a wild bird, such a thing of the natural world, should be set free and its political reference seems to hover. *Dreaming for Joy* makes this more concrete perhaps: another bird, a huge crow in brilliant red buttons, its beak, head and most of its breastbone intact, buttons from wings, feathers and feet disintegrating, fall to the floor. Its head is bent tight round the corner of a huge steel cage, and behind a spectral image in white, mirrors the shadows cast by each button, as if death or doppelgänger is at hand. As viewer you can walk into the cage, scoop up the buttons and let them fall as you will. Despite this inherent serious intent, the red crow is full of vivacity, light catapulting off its shimmering pinion. At the Asian Contemporary Art Fair where it was exhibited in New York in 2008, sometimes the steel bars of the cell were left closed, so that the playful image seemed incarcerated beyond reach.

Today the bulk of modern buttons comes from China. Those used in Hwang's work are not pearlies' mother-of-pearl, nor the fine fashion buttons still trickling out of Italy. In the early twentieth century the Italian industrial district of Val Calepio, or 'Button Valley', managed to capitalize on its craft tradition and capture large swathes of the market. It developed the relatively new corozo, a material made from a dense albumen extracted from the seeds of the American palm tree, which could be dyed to any colour and after baking could be chiselled like stone. Still the finer quality modern buttons come from Italy, but the mounting demand for clothes, ever-more new and throwaway, creates a monster – this time not the child-labour and dangerous working conditions of a Birmingham factory, but the overwhelming economic machine of China's factory system.

The small town of Qiatou, with its 200 factories and 20,000 migrant workers, is said to provide about 60 per cent of the world's supply of buttons. An apocryphal story emerged a few decades ago about three brothers who notice the way buttons are discarded without a backward glance. They realize money is to be made from such carelessness and pick up any buttons they can find and start to resell them, and ... hey presto, the button town is born.

The modern button industry in China offers largely low-skilled and low-waged work so that as people's expectations grow, a labour shortage is emerging. While conditions may improve for some workers, the danger lies in the pressure to find new sources of workforce. World commodity prices soar and the price of copper buttons coming out of China, for example, doubled in 2008. There are reports of child-labour being the norm for the more repetitive tasks, which, together with unsafe factory conditions, enables the sure supply of cheap buttons to the West. Despite recent official regulations banning the employment of anyone under 16, it is easy to see how poorer people from rural areas are driven to send their children to work in the new factories of the developing southern and coastal areas. They have always had to call on their children to help in the fields and now find that with the increased cost of schooling, they have limited options. Button factories involve the relatively light mechanical work for which small fingers and good young eyesight are ideally suited.

In recent history, the seductive cheongsam, with a row of small usually silk or satin covered buttons from neck to knee and, in contrast, the Mao Suit provide the West's most striking images of China. The former, in Western film at least, allowed one to think of Chinese women as willingly hobbled by their figure-hugging split-skirted narrow sheaths. Maggie Cheung wore over 20 different cheongsams in the film *In the Mood for Love* and created a lasting portrait of seduction and sophistication. The familiar People's Suit was actually designed and first worn by Sun Yat-sen. The influence of the Soviet Union's 'Lenin Coat' meant that some Chinese had their previously single-breasted suits made double-breasted. Even in hard times tailors were able to make a good living, even if it was just repairing old clothes or altering the buttons of such jackets.

In the Cultural Revolution the influence of military uniform made it inadvisable to wear anything too frivolous or too new-looking, so that it became the custom to break in new clothes to make them look respectably work-worn. In 1976 Pierre Cardin threw a fashion show in Beijing, updating and bringing colour to the blue, grey and black palette of revolutionary China. Recently, updated Tang-style suits were being worn at the APEC meeting in Shanghai, with younger people looking towards a non-Western, 'classical' idea of modern dress.

One story springs from Iran. A young Iranian woman based in London described how, returning to visit family, it was necessary to cover up with a headscarf and a modest dark coat, known as a *manteau*. Though a practising Muslim, she disliked this obligation and so chose to have the buttons on her *manteau* made extra large. Asked why this might be, she explained that it meant she could then remove it quickly, without fumbling. The more interesting reason was that other women, of a similar persuasion, would also be wearing larger buttons, and so they could recognize each other thereby. And there it was: buttons as secret signifiers on the streets of modern Iran. In fashion terms, what was intended to displace women's love of clothes provides a subtle means of fashion surviving as a discreet political gesture.

Western Australia produced the majority of mother-of-pearl buttons from the 1880s until the 1950s. The pearl oyster was at first harvested by forced-labour Aborigine divers, but later, as deeper beds had to be farmed and equipment therefore became necessary, Japanese divers were particularly highly valued. The work was dangerous, with the risk of drowning, the 'bends', box jellyfish, sharks and cyclones; yet the trade was so successful that the pearling town of Broome grew up, serviced by Chinese, Malayan, Filipino and Javanese workers. It was not the pearls found that created Broome's wealth so much as their by-product shells, and in particular their use for buttons. More recently, with competition from Japanese sources and the plastic button, Broome has turned its hand to cultured pearl production. The New Zealand dark paua shell (known also as abalone or ormer) is still used for buttons, with their distinctive blue-green iridescent surface.

Lastly, something must be said of the less hidden forms of button sign systems in the context of religious adherence and the complex business of clerical costume. The novelist Barbara Pym has a mother shocked by the ugliness of her priest-son's cassock, thinking he looks 'like some old monk'. Yet the cassock stops her mocking his success with women:

Perhaps the sight of the cassock silenced her, for she contented herself by pulling him towards her and telling him that one of the buttons was loose.

(*No Fond Return of Love*, 1961, p. 160)

Clerical costume has a long history of sumptuous dress, with fine buttons often the final decorative flourish. Since the position of priest has tended to give worldly as well as spiritual status, the early Christian church struggled to enforce codes of modesty and quiet dress on its clergy. As early as 1215 the Fourth Lateran Council insisted upon distinctive dress for the clergy, the avoidance of fine costume and in particular advised that clothes should reach to the shin, or at the least be long enough to keep the knees covered. Clergy were to wear garments closed in front, not tight-fitting and that should be free from extravagance: *clausa deferant desurper inclumenta*. The decrees became numerous, which suggests they were not so very successful. It is easy to understand why a priest, monk or nun, spending long hours in cold damp churches, perhaps in night offices, might long for a fur-lined hooded cloak, but also important is the association with authority and respect attached to sumptuous costume, bearing lavish buttons. A National Council of English Clergy in 1237 declared that the laity were being scandalized by priests wearing tunics or copes more suited to knights than clergy: *non clericalis sed potius militaris*.

In the Middle Ages, attempts were made throughout Europe to inhibit clerical tastes for fine fabric, rich adornment and for sumptuous vestments, and the penalties could be severe, risking ex-communication, heavy fines or losing title to their benefices. A Roman decree of 1708 suggests that, concerning the short cassock or the *pernique*, clerics should not only cover their knees, but also avoid large buttons. In the mid-twentieth century Anglican bishops started to wear purple (or violet) buttoned shirts as a sign of office, but there remains the feeling that it might be considered self-aggrandizing for any more lowly clergy to do so.

Cassocks, or soutanes, have a row of usually small covered buttons down the front opening and are worn by Roman Catholics, some Reform and Lutheran clergy, the Eastern Orthodox and the Anglican Church, and derive from the tunics worn beneath togas in classical Greece. In the Catholic version the 33 buttons are said to represent the years of Jesus's life; in the Anglican the 39 buttons represent the 39 Articles of Faith. The Ambrosian cassock has only five buttons, with a broad sash at the waist; the French cassock has buttons elegantly up the sleeves as in a modern lounge suit; Jesuits prefer a fly fastening and no buttons on show whatsoever. Though the predominant colour may be black, there remains some lingering evidence of former exuberance, in the rules of appropriate trimmings. A bishop may have amaranthine buttons, piping and sash; a cardinal scarlet. A pope even of today may sometimes vie with a Doge of Venice for fine damasked vestments and gorgeous gilded and embroidered rows of buttons. The cassock itself, however, remains ambiguous apparel, denoting simplicity and otherworldliness, but the fine cut and silk fabrics used by some priests may betray a degree of worldly vanity.

On a woman, a dress in the style of a cassock denotes a desire for modesty and lack of feminine furbelows, even a sense of family values, as with George Eliot's Mrs Meyrick, the small half-French mother-figure of Quakerish costume, whom Daniel trusts with Myra Lapidoth's care:

... her black dress almost like a priest's cassock with its rows of buttons ...

(*Daniel Deronda*, 1884, ch. 18)

The priestly biretta too, that three or four-part ridged folding squared cap, is finished off by a large tufted button on the top, black for regular clergy and scarlet for a cardinal, and so on. It was formerly worn for giving absolution in the confessional, but today is more likely to be used by traditionally minded clerics for outdoor services. However this connection with judgement and retribution forms a link, perhaps, with similar headgear used in the law courts, including the blackcap that was worn to pronounce death sentences. The same medieval ancestry has developed into the mortarboard now used mainly in university degree ceremonies, though the tufted button has become a mere tassel. Saints have been depicted wearing the biretta to demonstrate their learning, including St Teresa of Ávila and St Thérèse of Lisieux, and it is worth mentioning here that buttons of the saints have long been collected as holy relics.

Much as the influence of the cute, of war, death and religion have been important in the development of the button, there has been another vibrant area that, along with modern psychoanalysis, the power of advertising and the rise of the gender issue, has dominated our response to the world and which is exemplified by the course of the modern button.

CHAPTER EIGHT

Sex, Love and Buttons

Ellen: What would you men do if there were no women around to sew your buttons on?

Alec: Without women we wouldn't need any buttons!

(Fritz Lang, *Human Desire*, 1954)

In the arena of romance, there is a great difference between the totemic and the functional significance of the button. If buttons can be sexy, this is usually more to do with what they are hiding, or very nearly hiding, than anything in the make-up and design of the button itself. For a button to be romantic, or serve a romantic purpose, it more often than not plays a rather passive role, as something to be contemplated, perhaps recalling an absent beloved, or garnered from a would-be lover. A button is small enough to be able to carry discreetly on a chain about your neck or you might just finger it, deep in a pocket as the object of your desire walks unaware of your red hot passion, your manic fixation, your undying devotion. But buttons were not always seen as playing a token role.

Hair buttons were not only used as *memento mori*, but also as amorous talismans, for the idea of possessing a portable sample of a lover's body can be seductive, and hair is more fragrant than a cherished toe nail, with better prospects than a head stored in an olive jar. Hair might be handed over to a craftsman and woven into fine buttons, then given as a gift to one's object of desire, or one might oneself wear the lover's hair fetish. Sometimes the token might be taken without their being aware, and carried secretly in a locket button, magically to induce their affections – or, in an echo of Samson and Delilah, to reduce their powers of resistance, perhaps.

Those made as romantic tokens, or to invite flirtation, include some of the finest eighteenth and nineteenth-century buttons, with delicately painted scenes on enamel, ivory and paper, often encrusted with jewels or surrounded by polished steel and glowing copper rims. A plain plastic button may, of course, carry a weight of romantic longing, but there are also examples of the exquisitely fashioned, intended to bestow romance upon the wearer. There are the more blatant scenes of lovers, some tender, some erotic, some just cute, or the subject may be treated more symbolically.

Flowers, for example, were a way of surreptitiously sending a lover's message: daisies and lilies for innocence or purity; carnations for betrothal, and in China for marriage. In India such buttons might have jasmine for love; juniper promises chastity; mistletoe a kiss; and roses are central to this catalogue, with red for passionate love, white for virginity and yellow spelling jealousy and infidelity. A present of sunflower-embellished buttons should make one wary, symbolizing a foolish passion, one's head turning infatuated wherever the all-powerful sun/lover moves in its orbit. Cupid (or Eros) also appears, sometimes the dangerous, fickle, winged boy, sometimes a cheeky cherub in nappies. He holds a quiver of arrows and bow, one arrow perhaps tipped with a heart, ready to make people fall in love, or sometimes simply overwhelm them with sexual desire.

The conventionalized symbol of a heart occurs frequently, sometimes forming the overall shape of the button; more implicitly the symbol of the moon is a troubling one, suggesting night's passion, yet in its waxing and waning it mimics love's mutability and so fickleness and transgression. There are moon buttons of mysterious beauty made of mother-of-pearl, ivory and silver, often in mixed media: silver moon on ivory sky; mother-of-pearl for its translucence with inlay of gold; deep blue enamel firmament laid guilloché on a silver ground, revealing a moon, impassive or with knowing grin (see examples in Epstein and Safro, 1991). The figure of Harlequin (derived from commedia dell'arte), the foppish lover of Columbine, in diamond-patterned tights and black mask, represents a sometimes comic but ultimately more mortal, fallible love. Animals too, more often a pet dog, were used to express a message of loyalty and devotion (see Chapter 3).

Lord Byron, that brooding romantic figure of English poetry, had buttons made with his family motto: 'Crede Byron', as in 'Byron is an honest man of his word'. It is said that Mary Shelley mischievously had an alternative set emblazoned: 'Non Credo Byron' or 'He is a Liar'. Not a very romantic gesture perhaps, but it highlights the difficulty buttons have in being taken entirely seriously, with the gravity that sincere till-death-do-us-part passion tends to require, whether that message is implicit or explicit. Buttons manage much more ably to suggest sexual love, or perhaps the more superficial idea of the sexy.

Straightforwardly, buttons are to do with dressing and undressing. Underclothing, for those of means, once involved legions of small linen-covered, satin and silk-covered, or pearl buttons on bodice, camisole, undershirt, gusset, the flies of long johns and early underpants. Buttoned corsets, or stays as they were called, were worn as early as the sixteenth century. Gradually, the construction became more elaborate, with whalebone, wood and steel reinforcements required as the structures became more engineered. While the back was laced, the front opening, or busk (a term also applied to the strips of whalebone), was buttoned and/or hooked together for easier removal.

In the nineteenth century the race was on for women to achieve the smallest waist possible, thus emphasizing the chest, bottom and hips. For women, unbuttoning a corset becomes a sexually feminine and also potentially fetishized act. In contrast, for a man the business of unbuttoning his corset might normally hold little sexual allure. To have been seen to wear a corset at all, he might have to claim medical need, even if he was in reality simply attempting to hide middle-age spread. For a brief period until the mid-nineteenth century, the corset was sometimes adopted by the dandy, as it had been by the fop before him, as a fashionable underpinning to achieve a wasp-waisted silhouette. After the 1850s any self-respecting man would rather be suspected of back pain or even hernia than admit to such vanity. In a woman its removal provides release that allows her more freedom of movement, so potentially greater acrobatic possibility. On the other hand, a corset need not impede sexual congress and retains its erotic hold on the imagination, offering something both restricted yet still available.

A young woman's first girdle was a right of passage into adulthood. Despite the revolution in women's underclothing in the 1960s, many continued to wear girdles, just as some had not left off their stays despite the free-form 1920s. I recall wearing a fleecy liberty bodice at school in the 60s, buttoned and with pairs of dusty pink rubber buttons attached for optional suspenders – hardly cutting-edge, yet as androgynous as I was, it felt distinctly grown up.

The corset has been worn as outer wear, in the post-Second World War New Look as a type of cinched belt, and in the 1980s and 1990s it was developed by designers such as Christian Lacroix, Vivienne Westwood and Antonio Beradi and popularized by the pop singer Madonna, becoming a cliché of sexy clothing and the staple wear of current trend-setters such as Lady Gaga. Yet, as a fetish, the corset retains something of its erotic role as a garment of submission, where the subject is forced to wear what is unpleasantly restrictive. Alison Lurie makes the point that clothes, if they are anything like a sentence, 'can mean more than one thing at a time' (1981, p. xi). Madonna's pop-diva stance takes on the garb of the victim female and then delightedly attempts to reverse its meaning. But the sense of something private being exposed remains. She becomes its manipulator, but also arguably becomes knowingly complicit in a form of the degradation of women, and significantly of herself.

Corsetry may be adopted by both genders in sadomasochistic practice as dominant garb, the usually black carapace making the wearer look and feel more powerful. While the introduction of rubber in undergarments allowed for greater comfort, leading to the stretchy, button-free roll-on girdle, in the area of sadomasochism it has provided greater skin-fitting, impenetrable possibilities. The rubber button is enjoyed both for its ability to button securely and its being extremely difficult to unbutton. The leather button is also

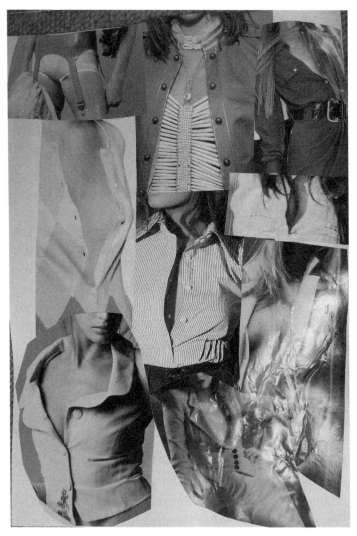

30. Nellie Collier collage, *How's Your Father*, 2009.

a resonant feature, with an appeal to the primitive perhaps, but possibly more to do with its feel of skin against skin. Fur buttons used on fur coats, particularly in the twentieth century, also found their way into the pornographic lexicon, suggesting something of an animal pelt, of savagery, but also of decadent luxury and implicitly those hidden hairy parts of the human body.

In popular culture, blonde bombshells and sultry brunettes alike are pictured with buttons straining over heaving chests:

> Granny: Ellie May done popped the buttons off her shirt again.
>
> (*The Beverley Hillbillies*, CBS, 1962)

Linda Grant points to the readily understood semaphore of the carelessly undone button (2009, pp. 92–3), and in like manner the button that is apparently absent-mindedly stroked and fiddled with is a common and sometimes unwitting means of flirtation. Buttons provide the illusion of promise but in reality may be merely a tease, or possibly disguise something less than wholly appealing. Some would say that this is the job of well-designed clothes in general: to promise delight until it is too late to politely decline.

Men, particularly when shirts are worn fitted, may seem to have chests so muscular, so swollen from manly exertion that their buttons are constantly under threat, like some version of the Marvel Comics' Incredible Hulk, a superhero who, when cornered, is taken over by a fearsome alter ego, impulsive and impassioned, shirt ripping, buttons bursting free. While fashion may dictate T-shirts or less fitted shirts at times, the idea of a muscularly developed male chest has retained its erotic pull, how-soever leanness, all-over tattoos, piercings or the hirsute may take one's fancy. Unlike the more obvious signage of the promise of imminent exposure of female breasts, the less obvious, tertiary rather than secondary characteristic perhaps of a male torso, might be said to allow a more gradual and thus seductive allure. It is less available to feelings of prurience, albeit that all parts of the body may in the right circumstances offer such promise. Robert Frost's poem 'A Hundred Collars' has two men sharing a room:

> He sat there creased and shining in the light
> Fumbling the buttons in a well-starched shirt.

> (Robert Frost, 'A Hundred Collars', 1915)

This is not an overtly sexual moment, yet 'fumbling' and 'buttons' in close proximity obliquely introduces erotic possibility between the two men. One of the most debated scenes in British television drama of the late 1990s is that of the Andrew Davies's adaptation of *Pride and Prejudice*, where Elizabeth Bennett happens upon the nor-mally restrained Darcy. He has been swimming in a lake, and although fully dressed in modern terms, his billowing shirt catches on his still-damp torso, the buttons strain-ing against the distorted wet buttonholes. That they do stay done up arguably invests the moment with increased sexual tension. As both attempt polite conversation, we see Elizabeth's eyes glance down, taking in the details of Darcy's body, a man whom she had recently roundly rejected. Davies provides a poignant filmic means for

Elizabeth to admit to herself her desire for Darcy, when she believes it is all too late.

The fashions of Jane Austen's time, at the very end of the eighteenth century and the beginning of the next, are particularly unbuttoned for females, with the emphasis on a classical, draped simplicity; male style has withdrawn from the height of eighteenth-century display, with Brummell-influenced simple gilt buttons and the new buttoned proto-trousers, in which we see Darcy silhouetted in his glory, as he undresses for a swim. However, from about the 1830s fashion and attitudes undergo a radical change. Women's gussets, for example, became buttoned rather than open and the relation between buttoning, unbuttoning and physical passion is reinforced. It seems that buttons or the lack of them may both be read as erotically charged. For men the buttoned fly takes on a parallel role. In the Renaissance period men of fashion had open groins covered by a codpiece, and later breeches would do up with a flap, buttoning or tying at the waist. The modern buttoned fly opening was convenient for urination but, as trousers became tighter in the 1950s, they also allowed a sexually suggestive close fit.

Riveted vintage Levis are of greater value if they carry the 'Big E' motto on the fly buttons. The idea of sexual availability became associated with the easily unbuttoned fly. Elvis Presley in close-fitting 501s, gyrating, hips swivelling, gave us the apotheosis of the fly. Some critics likened his first television performance of 'Hound Dog' to a striptease, and the act brought about his nickname of Elvis the Pelvis. His crotch area was largely censored on the *Ed Sullivan Show*, but as he slid on his knees towards the camera, fly buttons to the fore, what could not be seen took on a far greater erotic significance. As jeans began to be worn by both genders, some of this sexual dynamic deserts the button fly.

Undone buttons are the stuff of knock-about comedy. Ogden Nash, in his *PG Woodhouse, Just as he Useter*, cries dangerously: 'Flourish the fish slice, your buttons unloosing'. A. A. Milne warns more whimsically in *Twice Times* that 'bad bear (has) left all his buttons undone'. Both comedy and humiliation are associated with the fly accidentally left open. Winston Churchill, when warned of such an oversight, is said to have rejoined, 'dead birds do not drop out of nests'. Of the many euphemisms used in this context the Irish expression 'You have egg on your chin' somehow springs to mind, presumably aping the anxious downward glance a man might make to check his flies.

Liberation might be seen in terms of Erica Jong's 'zipless fuck' (*Fear of Flying*, 1973), but the zip, and latterly the pull-on sports' trouser, reduced the buttoned fly practically to the position of fogeyish affectation. In the 1970s the covers of pop music albums for groups like Velvet Underground and Andy Warhol's image of tight jeans for the Rolling Stones' *Sticky Fingers* proclaim the erotic power of the zip in denim. But as ever in such sartorial matters, things have come full circle and the fly button has returned to the biting edge of fashion and Big E jeans are again in high demand. The Stones may have fully engaged with the image of the zip, yet their cover version of the 1960s Rufus Thomas classic can still suggest the sexual potency of the button:

Baby back
Dressed in black
Silver buttons all down her back...

(Rolling Stones, 'Walking the Dog', 1964)

31. Button flies.

There is, of course, much shifting ground between the romantic and the sexy. Just as desire was said to grow out of a chastely forged marriage, so there are examples of romantic feelings following on from button-popping orgies of delight. Porn stars may fall tenderly and enduringly in love, as in Paul Thomas Anderson's 1997 *Boogie Nights*. There must sometimes have been such ambition in pornographic buttons. There are examples displaying various sexual positions and series of men with exaggerated phalluses. A man might wear such buttons to amuse his friends or titillate a potential partner, and even in the hope of engendering true love. The eighteenth-century Georgiana, Duchess of Devonshire, reports to her mother an embarrassing moment on seeing the oversized pornographic buttons of the Duc de Chartres's waistcoat in 1783, describing them as:

> ...very indecent buttons, which my sister very near died of, as she said: 'quelle Grande boutons', without knowing what they were...

> (Bessborough (ed.), *The Correspondence of Georgiana Duchess of Devonshire*, 1955)

French prostitutes in the late eighteenth century had the habit of wearing small, crocheted buttons, or 'knobs' as they were known, on their blouses to advertise their trade on the boulevards and distinguish them from non-professionals. A 'slut who eats buttons' is a graphic metaphor for a streetwalker. It is the French who have refined the art of the pornographic button. Loic Allio has brought together a cache of eighteenth-century sexually explicit buttons: refined miniature scenes of shameless exhibitionism, showing different positions, mostly between men and women; blue enamel, more primitive in style; all manner of cast and moulded brass buttons illustrated with a naked woman urinating (after Rembrandt), naked wrestlers, an erect penis in the guise of a horse and another not at all erect and looking down despondently (entitled 'Les âges de la vie'), and a series of exquisitely fashioned pudenda.

The button has also played its part in striptease, some of the most edgy involving nothing but the unbuttoning of gloves and their slow removal. In a scene from Charles Vidor's film-noir *Gilda* (1946), femme fatale Rita Hayworth taunts both audience and husband as she slides off each black satin tube. She gives the impression that she will remove all – but a suggestion of 'unbuttoning' is sufficient to excite her audience. The mousquetaire glove has an opening at the wrist to allow the hand to be slipped out for dining and other practical purposes, without having to take the whole glove off. Sarah Bernhardt is said to have worn long mousquetaire gloves on stage, to hide her rather thin arms and draw attention to dramatic gesture. Conversely, long mousquetaires may hold firm ageing upper arms, so cruelly nicknamed 'bingo wings'.

Mousquetaires are said to derive from the buttoned gauntlets worn by French musketeers of the sixteenth and seventeenth centuries. The small section of wrist that may be glimpsed through the opening – that moon of paler pulsing flesh – could become a focus of erotic attention. Traditional mousquetaires carry three pearl buttons alone. The length of women's evening gloves are referred to in terms of 'buttons' whether they actually have them or not, those reaching to the elbow being 16 button, to mid-biceps 22 buttons and full shoulder-length are 30 button.

There can be very different sorts of suggestiveness in unbuttoned clothes. In Piero della Francesca's Renaissance altarpiece of a pregnant Madonna the buttons that open over Mary's stomach are not sexy in the modern sense, but wholly and seriously sensual. She holds her hand over the opening, as if to protect it from our gaze and so draws our attention to the centre of the painting, the creation of new life. Many seventeenth and eighteenth-century portraits of men are shown slightly unbuttoned at the waist, suggesting a certain softening of ageing flesh. Earlier sixteenth- and seventeenth-century examples, when a portrait might be to display the prestige of the sitter, offer opportunities to display a rich lace shirt beneath.

One might construe the button in terms of the theory of oral drive formulated by French psychoanalyst and psychiatrist Jacques Lacan. Lacan compares the way language is 'anchored' to symbolic meaning to *points de capiton*, or the buttons that reinforce a mattress, but quite what this reveals is unclear. Freud was much taken up with the possible meaning of buttons in his dreams, and in particular those left undone or that had accidentally come undone. Are they an unconscious form of invitation; clearly they can be just a careless oversight. As far as one's own attractiveness is concerned, one does not necessarily intend what others find attractive, any more than one can recognize what others find less than appealing. The deliberate seducer needs to maintain a level of objectivity that eludes most people in this most vulnerable sphere of interaction.

Buttons are nipple-like and in that sense make a deep-rooted demand on the onlooker, reminding them of babyhood, of the mother's breast, offering a partial manifestation of desire. From the end of the seventeenth to the end of the nineteenth centuries female breast-shaped buttons had been made in Holland and Norway. These buttons are not blatantly sexual, made of silver in the main, and often enhanced with floral and geometric designs. It is more perhaps that the button lends itself to so natural a shape. Many of the Navajo silver buttons are very similar in design and achieve the same sense of simple beauty.

In the language of pornography at least, buttons are exploited as a recurrent metaphor (see Chapter 1). For instance, 'to press the button' is to stimulate the clitoris or massage the prostate gland with finger or penis. A passive male partner is said to 'have his button pressed' or pushed by a male partner. 'Button mushroom' can be a pejorative term for a man.

Buttons have their place in domestic life, too. A womanly woman came to be associated with the sewing on of buttons. In the novel, *Germinal*, the hero feels loved because a woman tends to his domestic needs, his:

> ...laundry was washed and mended, his buttons were sewn back on and his things tidied. In short he could feel the benefit of a woman's touch.

> (Émile Zola, *Germinal*, 1835, pt. 3, ch. 3)

An unmarried man might have no reasonable expectation of keeping his buttons in good standing. During the 1950s silver-plated charms were sold to hide in Christmas puddings. Christmas can often be a cruelly droll time of year for the single, and there is pathos and intended mockery in silver shirt button charms being described as 'bachelor buttons'. Jo, the lively tomboyish heroine of *Little Women*, who at first baulks at the traditional expectations of her gender, is brought to marriage and to give up her writing ambitions by what she sees as Professor Bhaer's domestic need of her:

> ...he looked like a gentleman, though two buttons were off his coat...

And a little later she reflects:

> ...it was a little pathetic...to think of the poor man having to mend his own clothes. The German gentlemen embroider I know – but...

> (Louisa M. Alcott, *Good Wives*, 1880, ch. 10)

When marriage is beginning to lose its first romance, then the woman may be less assiduous and the husband more critical. T. S. Arthur describes the small tensions that may be expressed through buttons. His character Mr Jones, who has been married for some time, remarks to himself, 'I'd given up hoping for a shirt with a full compliment of buttons', and more sadly, 'there was a time in my married life ... when I was less annoyed if my bosom or wristband happened to be minus a button'. He decides to bear such absences 'like a martyr' – so it is hardly surprising that his lady wife mildly complains:

> I wish somebody would invent a shirt without buttons.

> (T. S. Arthur, *Trials and Tribulations of a Housekeeper*, 1859, ch. 10, 'Shirt Buttons')

The button seems to be a cause of mutual marital dissatisfaction, evoked by expectations of the female, including on occasion what women themselves feel should be their nurturing role. But women sometimes take a firmer line. George Eliot railed against all dressmakers, 'cursed be they in their needles and pins, cursed in their hooks and buttons' (cited in Crompton, 1960). In the 1950s Sylvia Plath was irritated by the idea that being a woman meant she ought to provide domestic support for her husband, Ted Hughes:

> I'm not 'sewing on buttons and darning socks by the hearthside'. He hasn't even got us a hearth; I haven't even sewed a button.
>
> (*Journals of Sylvia Plath*, p. 445)

And Ronald Hayman describes how,

> If they argued about buttons she hadn't sewn on to his jacket, the conflict was rooted in her attitude to the conventionality of his ideas about women.
>
> (Ronald Hayman, *The Death and Life of Sylvia Plath*, 2003, p. 116)

Plath has come to stand for women's feelings of resistance to the traditional role of fulfilling the domestic needs of a man. There is a certain irony here for accounts suggest Plath was not only dedicated to her craft but also someone who enjoyed domesticity and so might be said to represent the tug of allegiances often experienced by modern women. Yet in her poem for three voices, 'Three Women', there is a sense of desolate betrayal and refusal to submit to what is expected of her gender:

I shall not be accused by isolate buttons
Holes in the heels of socks

('Three Women', 1962, ll.138–9)

There are less politically charged, ambiguous aspects of the domestic button. Whatever your gender, if you have ever had to iron a shirt, you might recognize the quiet fact that buttons demand to be taken into consideration, and even then they may leave their imprint deep in the fabric of your task, an iron making:

the hiss
under each button

(Marsha Truman Cooper, *Ironing after Midnight*, 1990)

Some early electric irons carried a two-pronged device to help with ironing around buttons, but it could be cumbersome and awkward to use, stabbing the cloth – the button refusing to be easily managed – and are only found commercially today.

It has been necessary to talk of buttons in quite conventional gender-delineated roles, yet they have always been capable of expressing sexual ambiguity. Some women wore men's suits as a high fashion conceit in the period between the two world wars – just think of the elegant swagger of Marlene Dietrich. For some it was an opportunity to experiment with the idea of greater sexual freedom, for others merely a way of being madly fashionably shocking.

SEX, LOVE AND BUTTONS • 199

Chanel had introduced a style of masculine clothes that somehow heightened a woman's femininity – for example, the too-large man's jacket worn by a woman to show how fragile she is, suggesting how unlike the man for whom it was tailored she remains. I recall reading in *Vogue* as a child that to wear an oversized jacket was to seem to be in the embrace of a powerful man. Alison Lurie suggests (1981, p. 229) that the much-copied Annie Hall look of wearing actual men's clothing several sizes too big (after the 1977 film of the same name) allowed Diane Keaton to send a double message: that she was both happy-go-lucky tomboy and, though expressed as a more hidden suggestion, helpless, requiring a man's support, even one as 'incompetent...as the characters played by Woody Allen'. There is also the risk of looking like a female bouncer.

The difference between the single and double-breasted suit can make or mar an intended impression. The single-breasted jacket has only a narrow overlap, and a single column of buttons of usually two, three or four in a traditional man's jacket, and there can be more buttons on a woman's. In contrast, the double-breasted, never recommended to the short man or one hoping to disguise his girth, gives the woman who wears it greater possibilities of displaying her supposed relative weakness. The wide overlap allows a front panel and a double column of buttons, which may be continued up into the shoulders to increase their impression of breadth. Whereas an inner parallel-fastening button, or jigger, keeps the two sides in place, those on the outside should not come under strain in the well-made jacket. Only one column of buttons functions, the other being purely decorative.

The buttons on modern suits and blazers are referred to in tailoring by a numeric schema, the total number of buttons, followed by the number that actually fasten. Thus the typical four-button jacket, as worn by the Duke of Kent, known as a Kent, is a 'four-on-two'. Coats, too, can be single or double-breasted, the historical association with men's military overcoats remains in trench coats, pea coats and duffles. Fashion may play with the idea of a woman in masculine military uniform; similarly, a man in a single-breasted, easy-to-leave-open style may suggest something of feminized frailty.

The sense that buttons can evoke affection and may signify love and sexuality naturally brings them to the attention of artists. In all the spheres so far discussed art has played its part, in both the development of the button itself and as a meaningful material constituent in craft-based work.

CHAPTER NINE

Arts and Crafts

At the opening of each installment of the Jane Austen BBC television adaptation of *Pride and Prejudice* in 1995, there is a close-up of lace, satin and brocade, a hand poised with needle and thread, and fabric-covered buttons. We gather that this is a female world and that buttons are in its midst. The majority of artists who choose to work directly with buttons seem to be women, often bridging the hiatus between art and craft. There are those for whom buttons play a more peripheral role, but seem to have some significance in their work nonetheless. Some use buttons in such a way that they are hardly recognizable as such.

The potter Lucie Rie went into button production soon after her arrival in London in 1938, escaping Nazi Austria. Although she did so in order to make ends meet, her striking modernist designs and colour sense set a lasting standard for ceramic buttons. Her friend the gallerist Anita Besson told me how fashion designers would visit Rie with swatches of cloth and that she would then experiment with glazes until the right effect was reached. I was shown early handmade buttons which bore the print of her thumb, as she had pressed the clay concave. Later she made moulds to speed up production, but these more uniform buttons lack something of the intimate personality of the entirely hand-fashioned.

Whereas the majority of Rie's buttons are practical and can easily be imagined on the front of a simply cut jacket or swing coat, Besson prizes examples of miniature pot buttons, jugs and even a tiny cup in terracotta glazed with yellow – a nod towards Rie's work as maker of pots. The small studio, in converted stables off Hyde Park, where she worked for 50 years, has been reconstructed at the V&A and you can see there the moulds, a set of two, top and bottom, for each button design – reminding me disconcertingly of an oversized dental cast. A large collection of her buttons can be viewed by arrangement with the British Button Society, and others are held in the Farnham Crafts Study Centre archive. Both through her work and her teaching at Camberwell College of Art she has influenced generations of one-off and small production button makers.

Lucie Rie maintained friendships with her designers, notably in her latter years with Issey Miyake, who used her extraordinary organic buttons in his work. According to Besson, Rie was more interested in the challenge of producing suitable glazes for the buttons rather than the clothes for which they were intended. For his part, in 1989 Miyake included a line of clothing designed specifically with her buttons in mind, and Rie went on to bequeath to Miyake her personal button collection. In 2010 a retrospective of her work toured Japan, a country that continues to prize highly the work of the ceramicist.

The designer Kate Harris is a rare female influence on the art of the silversmith and though little is known of her apart from the legacy of her work, she was based at

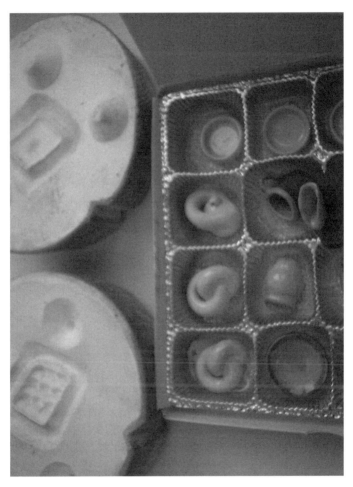

32. Ceramic buttons by Lucie Rie, housed for safekeeping in the lining of a chocolate box, beside their original moulds.

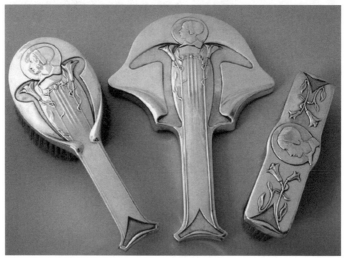

33. These fine silver Puritan Maid buttons match the dressing table set of mirror and brushes, which bears a maiden holding lilies with the same Puritan Maid heads. Designed by Kate Harris (1903 and '04) for Hatton and Sons.

Goldsmiths and Silversmiths Co. Ltd in 1899 and exhibited at the Paris Exhibition in 1900, under the auspices of Hutton and Sons, winning for them a prize for a tea set. Her style is a pared down Art Nouveau, suggesting the simplicity of the Arts and Crafts movement. I stood wondering at a boxed set of her Puritan Maid buttons, a design shown in profile, with a cap and two escaping tendrils of hair. The antiques' fair stall had a matching hand mirror, brush and clothes brush. Why would one want buttons to match such a set? A woman sits, one might imagine, at her dressing table before going out, in her silver Puritan Maid buttons. She would see herself in the mirror, brushing her hair perhaps and doing up her buttons, and might she not notice how they matched the beautiful silver pieces before her? No one else would ever have this view of the buttons' relation to the dressing table set, in this one single regard, an experience of refined and inconspicuous consumption:

But in her web she still delights
To weave the mirror's magic sights...

(Lord Tennyson, *The Lady of Shalott*, Part II, 1842)

One might imagine that beautiful and rare example of a William Morris painting, *La Belle Iseult*, at such an intimate moment of reflected self-contemplation.

Contemporary button makers are drawn from diverse fields. Trained jewellers may venture into buttons and find it suits them. Lucy Quartermaine produces deliberately pared-down plain silver buttons that she then transforms into restrained and elegant pieces, having been influenced by the touching button keepsakes at the Foundling Museum in London (see Chapter 3). They avoid seeming

34. Pared down elegance by Lucy Quartermaine, silver bracelet, 2009.

cute, as if something of their original inspiration remains. She has deliberately set out to use everyday objects and turn them into contemporary jewellery. Of her various designs, the button pieces, she explained, are some of the most popular, and she suspects that this is because the button 'is one of the only familiar shapes out there that is in everyone's lives, it is friendly and appealing... it has a smiley face on it'. Quartermaine, as her connection with the foundling tokens suggests, expresses this ambiguous aspect of the button through her work.

Laura Walker (Farrow) cites her experience as an embroiderer as a source of her button designs, and combines textiles in her work to produce works of unexpected texture and colour, commissioned by fashion designers and for art installations. Contemporary button producers, or *boutonniers* – for there does not seem to be an English language word for such – create a wide variety of Perspex and plastic buttons that bear little resemblance to the cheap and mass-produced: etched with colour and pattern, whirls of swirling colour to rival Venetian glass; cones of opaque resin studded with metal that Elizabeth I would have envied. Modern enamelware provides the depth of colour and spontaneous painterly design that so influenced the Arts and Crafts movement of the turn of the twentieth century.

There are of course many craftspeople who do not make their own buttons, for their art lies in the selection and construction of jewellery, as with Judith Brown who creates pieces out of hand-stitched silver wire like the finest filigree woven into antique mother-of-pearl buttons. She told me that it was early in her jewellery making career that she felt inspired by an intricate carved button in her mother's collection – drawing on her memories of being

35. Intricate hand-stitched silver wirework over vintage, carved mother-of-pearl buttons, giving the appearance of filigree. *Vintage button necklace*, Judith Brown, 2007.

taught to sew and the shared experience as mother and daughter concentrated on some sewing project together. Like Walker, a trained embroiderer, she saw an opportunity to use her newly acquired wire stitching technique, and this fascination with using old, discarded fastenings has also led her to make an unusual range using black hooks and eyes. She is consciously attracted to the notion of creating something from what is considered nothing: 'the buttons seemed precious as someone (probably my grandma) had taken the time to cut them off an old item of clothing and save it, putting it away to be reused at a later date'. Visit any major museum shop and you will glimpse the range of skilled craftspeople currently working with buttons using ceramics, wood, leather, metals, Perspex encased images that look back to the tintypes and even the eighteenth-century hand painted miniatures before them.

There are those who employ buttons as a constituent part of their ceramics, such as the potter Pam Schomberg, who explains (BBC Essex, 23 June 2009) that her father's having been a tailor has driven her to treat her pots almost like clothing, with apparent seams, collars, edges and buttons. Her *Crittall* tea service pieces are part weird architecture, part garment. Priscilla Jones, contrariwise, has made fabric tea cups, saucers and spoons that look like fine glazed porcelain seemingly held together with buttons. Her three-dimensional teapots are partly transparent, a glove finger forming a handle, the spout stitched into the metal framework beneath.

In both Schomberg and Jones this feature of one thing needing to be made to look like another seems crucial, as if the visual transformation forces the viewer to re-see the fabric of the world. Jones describes her fascination with the idea of Miss Haversham and the long ago jilted woman's decaying wedding feast in *Great Expectations* (1861) and Dickens's description of a 'phantom air of something that had been and was changed'. This sophisticated notion drives many artists who work with buttons.

Jones specifically links her work not only to a fictional image but to her own life: 'all my pieces are nostalgic in their essence and each one I create is related to a recollection or a memory' (Livesay, 2009). I think it is this sense of personal familiarity that urges so many of these artists to think about using the button. They notice something redolent with meaning and use their work to reframe it so that we notice too.

Beth Livesay locates Jones's attraction to using haberdashery directly in her childhood experience, and goes on to explain the artist's preference for using vintage materials. The buttons that decorate the side of a milk jug or the handle of an ice cream spoon supply the sort of detail that they might more conventionally provide for a piece of clothing. She also reflects that using scraps of the past in this way feels in tune with recycling and new thrift. Ann Carrington and Kate Kessling both site a deliberate desire to reuse what has been discarded, and the same objective fuels artists such as quilter Jane Burch Cochran (Chapter 6) and the Ethiopian artist Elias Simé (Chapter 7).

It seems that artists who use buttons are often drawn from, or influenced by, as in the case of Schomberg, the fields of dressmaking and tailoring. Just as the craft qualities of Charles Ledray's miniature clothes (Chapter 6) with his minutely carved bone buttons are central to the strange allure of his installations, so we look to the stitches in Jones's 'china'. Some use paper as their fabric, conspiring to convince us of their fabric, non-paper substance.

The French artist Elisabeth Lecourt uses maps to sculpt clothing, but this is an art of synchronized illusion. Partly one is lured by the magnetism of the globe and our associations with the different spheres she chooses to juxtapose. Conventional men's shirts and old-fashioned girls' party frocks are cut out and pleated, and we as audience grapple for meaning in a shirt with its neat paper buttons and its stuff of the Indian subcontinent. Is it Indian sweatshops set against corporate man, or might it be that we are just being shown how the shape of the landmass lends itself to an ideal male form? All is implicit. A frock from another age, frilly and prettily synthetic, of a birthday party perhaps in the 1960s or early 1970s, and it is made from modern rude, crude, Europe. The colours of the maps play their part, vibrant yellow and green sacrifice the more serious message that may have occurred to the viewer, or perhaps the initially cheerful impact is undercut by the context. One dress in plain cream is entitled '*Instructions on How to Cry*', another '*Trust Fund Girl*'. She calls her *Prisengracht* (a coat) a portrait, so we know she wants us to take it seriously, as something other than just a coat. Portraits, good portraits, should reveal their subject.

Jennifer Collier makes elegant high heels with frilly paper covered buttons, like a shoe for Marie-Antoinette. They seem at first merely charming. But sometimes they are made from old dress patterns, sometimes wallpaper, sometimes Swiss banknotes – so that once again one struggles to work out what this may denote: the craft, the bourgeois interior world, the relation between fashion and capitalism? All are up for grabs. We are drawn in by the beauty of these fragile artefacts. Both Lecourt and Collier put me in mind of the delight once felt in paper cut-out dolls and their cut-out clothes, brilliant on the back cover

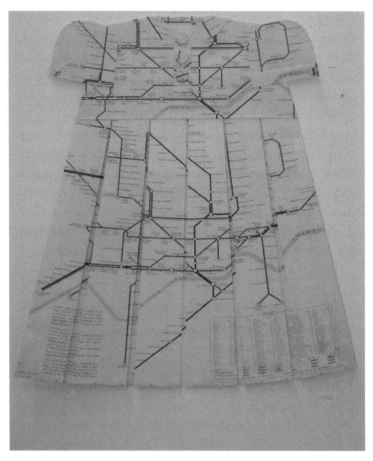

36. *Coccinelle Demoiselle*, map of the London Underground, Elisabeth Lecourt, 2009.

of a girls' *Bunty* comic. However, both these artists, despite the engaging imagery, of pretty frivolous shoes and party dresses, say, pose serious if implicit questions about the fragility of the physical world and our manipulation of it.

The Lecourt dresses remind me of the artist Grayson Perry's frocks, in both style and resonance. His alter-ego *Claire* wears full-blown little girl party frocks, often with large fancy buttons down the front, like a pantomime dame, which makes them seem even more childlike. Perry describes the look as that of 'a toddler at a wedding'. Each year he teaches a course at Central Saint Martins College in London, during which his students make Claire dresses which are awarded ceramic prizes, or 'Claires'. He describes (Copping, 2007) one of his favourites as having 'a quilted flared top with lots of little teddy bears that you can attach as buttons'. He remembers he was once keen on an 'all-buttoned-in-ness'. And Claire, he explains, is the kind of woman, 'who eats ready-made and can just about sew on a button'. Whatever the deep-seated reasons for his liking for the frocks, what is relevant here is his interest in button-ness and its effect on his feelings about personal identity, and more widely on the nature of his ceramic work. He finds meaning in the apparently jolly, the cutely buttoned-up-ness of it all. At the same time there is something more than playful going on, as if he intends to subvert an expectation of jolliness, with a dress, for example, depicting a head of Christ with ceramic buttons in a crucifix design. Perry is not a little girl, and as he gazes out from the many images the press captures of his Claire, he looks amused by the confusion he causes.

In E terminal of Atlanta airport you can find large-scale folk art, running up the walls and stairwells of what might otherwise be a bleakly familiar public space. The

curators wanted to encourage a sense of place and promote their regional culture. The artist Amalia Amaki
made a vast contemporary version of a buttoned quilt in
the skylight at Gate 5 entitled *Sojourners* (1996), depicting
a range of photographs of people, patchworked together,
famous and not. Lower down there are smaller works,
added in 1999. They seem at first to be unchallenging,
presenting one with familiar, often smiling faces, and with
domestic artefacts. But there is something more going on.
Quilts, for example, are by their nature warm and comforting, but also suggest melancholy. They can be made
up of remnants of old clothes, perhaps reminding of lost
youth, and of the dead. They represent a craft world that
has been suffocated by modernity. Amaki likes to use
the colour blue, which she intends in part as a connection with 'blues' music and her African-American background (Zak, 2005). Burn marks and iron scalds on the
photographs are meant to suggest the branding irons of
slavery. Buttons appear throughout her work, punctur-
ing and connecting the different layers of quilting and
decorating purses, fans and boxes of chocolates – which
recalled Anita Besson's personal collection of Lucie Rie
buttons, kept safe in the crenellated cups of a chocolate
box. Amaki likes her buttons to be second-hand:

> ...being touched by all these unknown hands...who
> knows how many hands touched a single button? At
> the same time they're very beautiful, ornate, like jew-
> els. They were at one time used as currency. So there
> are all these sort of wonderful histories embodied in the
> buttons.

(Carolyn Weaver, *Voice of America*, 14 July 2005)

Her exhibition 'Boxes, Buttons and the Blues' had chocolates that were decorated with buttons, and if you reached to take one an alarm was set off. She wants you to notice things are not as they might seem:

> (with) a lot of the candy, even the titles like 'Dark Chocolate' I am alluding to skin color and things like that. But it's not just a kind of racial reference. It's also talking about richness.

(Carolyn Weaver, *Voice of America*, 14 July 2005)

The exhibition included a wax cake decorated with buttons, and more immediately disturbing, nineteenth-century postcards of black children made to perform at the Moulin Rouge in Paris, but any unease Amaki character-istically undercuts by adding pieces of ornamental fabric and buttons. By withholding censure she allows one to see the works as aesthetic objects and for any tentative judge-ment to be one's own. The apparent function of quilts and boxes of chocolates encourages us to expect comfort and sensual pleasure, and it is a feat to allow us to go on enjoy-ing those associations while at the same time being asked to consider the more serious themes in her work.

Amaki's approach leads one to reflect on the business of using found objects in art. Ann Carrington, who produced the Pearly Kings and Queens discussed in Chapters 4 and 8, describes her joy in watching one thing become another. When she is not working with buttons, she is gathering spent shoes to make alligators, old boxing gloves are turned into a hare, evening gloves into a rabbit, pins and needles and cigarettes and most recently shells are transformed into crinolined ladies walking over a south coast English beach. This approach works on our imagination because of its appeal to childhood memory, and not only childhood, but the appeal of ordinary repeated minor experience that somehow adds up to the sum of many a life.

Of course the artists mentioned here are only a small sample of those who use the button in their work, and my main point has been to try to show how they capture the button in a way the collector does not – and yet their similarity in attitude has been marked. There is a pleasure in the quantity of buttons held and arranged by button collectors. As the old quip goes: enough is seldom as good as a feast. Artists who work with buttons will stress the amount they store and collate with a sense of glorious plenty. But what of vast works, that take up thousands of buttons? Carrington and Kessling talk of amassing buttons by the thousand. When their stocks are getting low, they become anxious. Ran Hwang, too, is concerned to express the quantities she needs, as if the more buttons she entertains, the more art is possible, her appetite fed by the idea of future so far unimagined work.

The relation between an artist's past experience and their work can make us feel as if we are in on the act; as if their biography is the key to aesthetic appreciation. The artist and sculptor Thomas Heatherwick admits to being the sum of his parents' and grandparents' influence. So is this past present in his arresting 30-metre high tumbling shower of a sculpture that towers, looms, scintillates, depending where you stand, filling a glass vaulted hallway in the Wellcome Trust building in London? There are 27,000 wires and 150,000 beads. Beads are not buttons, for they are older, more primitive, staunch cousins, yet seem to call on a very similar response in us. They have a purpose, albeit not a functional one. They are made for adornment, not to fasten. Like buttons they can be beautiful, valuable, sensual, cheap and cheerful, beloved by small children, full of sentiment or discarded as of no value. But these beads are doing something I had never seen before. I struggled for recognition. A great curving monument and yet light as air, as bubbles, twisting way above me. In the glass lift you get to see into this strange prism, as light ricochets off the myriad glass lozenges.

Then I remembered what I had learnt about Heatherwick's grandmother being a textile designer and Stephanie, his mother, running a bead shop, and my head began to clear. The sculpture is called *Bleigiessen*, which is an East European tradition involving foretelling the future from the curlicue shapes molten lead forms when it hits cold water. Heatherwick knew none of this. He had noticed the shapes liquid makes as it falls in gravity and experimented until he had settled on pouring molten white casting metal into water. Rather than design a suitable shape, he selected which chance casting would best suit the vault. His grand-mother had happened to be visiting his studio, seen the castings and immediately pronounced them *Bleigiessen*. It is not this interpretation alone, but the variety of possible interpretations, that seems to please Heatherwick.

Though the space was huge, the only entry point was a normal sized door, and he saw this not so much as a problem as an opportunity to make a vast whole from a multitude of small parts. In the film *The Ingenious Thomas Heatherwick* for the *Imagine* series for BBC 2 in 2006, Stephanie Heatherwick describes how her son had asked her about the making of an intricate beaded curtain that still hung at his childhood home. Again the link was being made between the sculpture and his past experience. Such biographical explanation is compelling, but there is a danger in thinking this is the route to summing up such an ambiguous, instinctive work of art. In some ways it might have been better to have remained in precipitous ignorance, and this may explain Heatherwick's refusal to wholly accept any particular interpretation.

It is hard to say unequivocally, but perhaps the button, because of its abiding utilitarian role in our lives, retains a sense of domestic proximity, which might have seemed too familiar; the bead can more easily distance itself. Bead and button can seem abruptly very different in resonance.

There are those who work with the idea of buttons in a way that has not previously been possible. Computer and digital technology have provided a new medium of virtual art. Ray Caesar works entirely with digital images: strange girls with transparent, almost raw skin, their often flimsy garments with buttons straining or tightly buttoned up to the neck, entrancing but often distorted, a world of classical beauty, manicured nature and weird deformity. His touch is light, full of strange humour, and some would say distinctly sinister. He too has a background that could be said to resonate in his pictures: for 20 years he worked in the art and photography department of a large children's hospital in Toronto. His job was to document the evidence of child abuse, psychological disturbance, photographing surgical reconstructions and animal research.

Against this gritty reality Caesar posits alternate surreal explanations, which seem to mock one's attempts to get a sense of him. Perhaps he became weary of all that knowing, possibly deferential, understanding – he grasps the problem with style. Consult the biography on his website and you will be confronted with the sad story of a man born as a dog who liked to draw on his stomach. His characters, he explains, are not influenced by sick children but the gift of 'a flesh toned 12 inch plastic movable human doll attired in cheaply made military fatigues called GI Joseph...'. In this account his mother, sympathizing with his canine difficulties, would sew outfits for the doll of, 'small business suits and leisure wear out of leftover Christmas fabric embroidered with holly and snowmen'. The joke is meant to pall: to test a greedy desire for biographic explanation perhaps. Eventually the page refuses to be further scrolled down, disappearing into the frame of the screen like the ornate frames in which he houses his prints.

Caesar is fascinated by clothing, and his buttons pull and gape, repress and reveal, taking centre stage in their glowing colours, brilliant cadmium yellow, lime greens, scarlet, puce and jet, his rococo doll-like figures peer at us, innocent or faintly disapproving, from their world apart. He mixes clothes of past gentility with modern medical prostheses, and metallic robot limbs. Some of the compositions are reworkings of classical paintings and thus, from a button perspective, the place they have in fashion is subverted. If a character looks both Edwardian and from some science fiction world, how does one place the buttons in history? For example, in Caesar's version of Eugène Boudin's *Woman with a Parasol on the Beach*, refined Parisian chic has to deal with tentacle legs, which he swathes in pretty, floral fabric tightly buttoned, multi-leg pantaloons.

They seem painted canvas, but the detail and clarity of the images with minute evenly distributed textures give them away as digital. If you want to see exactly what the buttons are, you can select and close up on the pixelated section. Like the beads in *Bleigiessen* or a single button in a Carrington, one can hone in on an individual constituent and they seem oddly separate. Caesar explains that:

...from its creation to its method of printing, I create models in a three dimensional modelling software and cover these models with painted and manipulated photographic textures and wrap around them like a map on a globe. Digital lights and cameras are added with shadows and reflections simulating that of a real world.

(www.raycaesar.com)

Kate Kessling has come to work with digital images, too. Her background is in fine art and textiles and at first her fascination with buttons led her to create 'sewn pieces' using large boards and drilling holes into them and then sewing the buttons on. It was a time-consuming and heavy-duty process, taking about six intensive weeks for each work and using 2,500 to 3,000 buttons a time. Lately she has learnt how to produce virtual images and describes that she now uses a combination of her original methods and 'photography to produce my images and I find I can work through and produce images more quickly, which I enjoy'. Certainly *Mourning Eye* (see Chapter 6) is a testament to her enthusiasm and attack.

Talking to Kessling brought me full circle in another way. Her description of how she came to be interested in buttons could have been my own, or that of any number of the button enthusiasts I have met: grandmother's button tin, childhood imagination, stories attaching to each button, a 'military uniform, a child's summer dress, a dead baby's cardigan. Each button', she explains, 'had a history and had become an artefact for the family archaeology' (Kate Kessling, pers. comm., 19 October 2009). Some of Kessling's oeuvre involves irregular patterns of similar buttons, spaced evenly as if for sale on a vintage button card. The detail of Caesar's work is present here too, in their high resolution, and that she calls them 'portraits' is revealing, playing with the idea of objects as abstract representations of the human face, some colourful and 'in your face' like her *Liquorice Buttons*, some more withdrawn, like an odd board game, as in *Noughts and Crosses*. I wondered if it could be button collectors who wanted these button pictures:

> It's fascinating just how interested people are in buttons. I get quite a response to my open studio events from people who spend hours looking through my buttons. Likewise I've had people with button phobia who feel literally sick at the thought of even coming into one of my exhibitions.
>
> (Kate Kessling, personal communication, 19 October 2009)

Collectors can be strangely resistant to the idea of art using the button. It seems to represent for them a form of adulteration that goes against the grain. They want to contemplate the details of a historically placed artefact, yet in the best art, the resonance of buttons is taken into account, even though the way that is done can be deliberately challenging.

The image of the button is a popular motif in textile design and does not seem to raise the same objections, perhaps because its marriage with fabric seems wholly appropriate, buttons being made for fabric. It is difficult to single out an example – but to end this chapter on an exuberant note, Zandra Rhodes created button themed textiles in the early 1970s which still seem joyously modern. She describes being attracted to the way the button maker J&J Stern displayed buttons, by attaching a little piece of pinked fabric between card and button, suggesting perhaps the zigzag motif that sometimes pervades her work. She contemplated simple geometric and flower-shaped buttons, which recalled for her the wavy flower motifs of Matisse. Out of this grew her Flower Button design, a button forming the centre of each flower, in turn reminiscent of the quilted yo-yos of embroidered quilting. Rhodes has documented the journey of each of her textile designs, and you can track the way initial drawing becomes paper mock-up, then fabric print in different colourways and finally the design for and garment itself.

> I thought I would draw the flowers like buttons stitched onto the fabric, the buttons being the flower centres with modern, bold Matisse shapes for the petals.

> (Zandra Rhodes and Anne Knight, *The Art of Zandra Rhodes*, 1995, p. 77)

She explained that to have her own actual button designs cast had proved prohibitive financially, and that she tended therefore to use loops and ties, embroidered covered buttons (see colour plate section), or sometimes dyed pearl beads. For the Button Flower textiles Mick Milligan designed button inspired jewellery. Her Dinosaur jacket and coat in felt is adorned with cut-out button-flowers at the shoulder and lined with the Button Flower print in satin; full satin dungarees bear a corsage of more button-flowers. She describes her fascination with the rich ornamentation of Fragonard and Boucher paintings in the

Wallace Collection, the 'wealth of detail; frills, buttons and bows, lace and flowers' – which brings this book full circle, when the great button makers of the Golden Age of the button, the eighteenth-century artists and *boutonniers*, drew on the very same sources of inspiration.

There remain a great many loose ends on this button exploration and it will be the job of the final chapter to attempt to gather these together and fasten off securely. Of course buttons are not by their sometime unbuttonable nature always suitable for such endings…

CHAPTER TEN

Dash My Buttons!
Alternatives, Buttonholes, Handmades, Badges, Furnishings, Virtuals, Bellybuttons

All this buttoning and unbuttoning

(Anonymous suicide note,
eighteenth century)

Buttons are not the only way to fasten a garment. While hooks and eyes may have given way to a more convenient form, today there is a range of possibilities and yet the button holds its ground. The most promising contender to take over its crown has to be the zip (Haldane, 2007). This has speed and cutting-edge design on its side, and is lean and dangerous as a snake. Patented by Elias Howe as early as 1851, a refined and more reliable version was first manufactured in 1913. Pilots during the First World War had zips fitted in their waterproof flying suits, but it was not until after the war that it began to be marketed to civilians. As late as the 1960s older British men still found the zip a touch ungentlemanly, alarmingly American in style. On the one hand early zips were prone to come undone, become misaligned or lose a tooth, and sometimes at the least convenient moments. Zips could stall. Nasty accidents might occur. If they break, the garment becomes unusable until the zip is replaced – unlike the loss of a single button.

Some considered zips to be vulgar, both morally and also in the sense of being associated with cheap or 'spivvy' clothing. The Forces were slow to allow their use in uniform trousers. They came to be associated with blatant eroticism. Children might get their fingers caught or be unable to line up the opposing rows in order to do them up, particularly in open-ended zips. On the other hand, they could be quicker and less fiddly, and nowadays buttoned trouser flies, unless say sewn on the outside of the placket as a design feature, are zipped. Two exceptions to this are the Hooray Henry tweedy look, worn to denote county conservatism in Britain, and in contrast, there are metal-buttoned jeans, both in their different ways referring to nostalgia for an aristocratic rural life and for the wide open prairies of the Wild West.

Zips are dynamic and fashion finds them thrilling. They were first made of metal, and gradually smoother running alloys were developed. From the 1930s plastics were used and, later, nylon. Zips made the low clicking or nibbling noise with their teeth that many find reassuring, sometimes sexy – recalling a scene in Mike Nichols's 1967 film *The Graduate*, where Mrs Robinson asks a nervous Benjamin to help unzip her. Schiaparelli was quick to design garments with prominently displayed zips, and she and Charles James began to use them in their couturier pieces.

Demonstrating great acumen, the designer arranged to be paid to promote them by their manufacturers, and was able to maximize her income by using different companies' zips, depending where her clothes were to be sold. In Paris and for export to the United States she employed Éclair, whereas in London she used the Lightning Company of Great Britain. However, it remains the case that some couturier houses continue to favour hooks and eyes, or buttons, over the zip, and this is certainly the case in many theatre and ballet costumes, where quick changes may mean that a zip can too easily fail.

Rather at the other end of the scale is the 'zipperless' zip, Velcro, the brand name for a type of hook and eye fastener, and now a universally useful fastening for sports clothes in general, for skiers and waterproof walking gear, for closures for bags and umbrellas and so on, but as an alternative to buttons on clothes, it has little charm. It is used by NASA on astronauts' space suits and to attach food pouches when there is no gravity. As against the zip, Velcro's teeth are small and snaggled and have little sensual potential. They might be used perhaps in the context of a strip-cabaret act, for example, but they are brash. The reveal is obvious and abrupt, as with the final moment of striptease in the 1997 Peter Cattaneo film *The Full Monty*, when red leather jockstraps are torn aloft. Compare that with Mrs Robinson's reveal and one can see what a difference a choice of fastening makes.

The most poetic fact about Velcro is its inception, as an idea springing from the way burrs attach themselves to dogs' fur. The extent to which it cannot injure the wearer or become broken matches its metaphorical impotence: the worst that can happen is for it to become clogged with nap and hair. The popper, press stud or snap fastener has more kinetic energy, but it has less flexibility. Velcro can be hastily attached or detached, but a popper relies on being right on target, and in many cases it may come apart under tension. But still the popper has an aura of charm and nostalgia about it that the rasp of Velcro lacks. One pulls deliberately upon a press stud and suddenly it comes apart, with a small glottal snap. The noise Velcro makes deems it unsuitable for men in close combat conditions; the enemy is unlikely to hear the button.

Jersey or stretchy fabric, rubber-based elastic and its more modern cousins, Spandex and Lycra, have to some extent made buttons even more of a deliberate decorative choice. Some people dislike wearing buttons: the jazz musician Duke Ellington, it is said, always preferred a pull-on shirt. Buttons may be hidden from view, as in the fly or in the parenthesis of a jacket placket: this mode of buttoning seems particularly grown-up, for the buttons are more difficult to get at, and yet the pleasure in the apparently unfettered closure and hidden presence of the buttons act as an elegant refinement.

Something should be said not for button substitutes, or improvements in the eyes of some, but for what buttons have been adapted to become. Buttons have been made into cuff links, brooches, rings and earrings, and diverse other bibelots, not to mention their use in decorative artworks. Although the market value of an eighteenth-century French reverse-painted button may be greatly reduced when it is so adapted, and moreover ruined as an aesthetic object for the purist, I would like to argue for another sort of value. For some, old clothes, even those marked with signs of wear, have a resonance that garments more cared for lack. A button that is no longer 'clean' may nonetheless become again an object both beautiful and useful. The serious collector may abhor imperfection, apart from that gentle patina of age that accrues around a valued object. They may not argue for a simple and elegant unity of form and function, but to see the button shank removed and replaced with a brooch pin may seem to them to betray its sense of integrity. However, it might be said that the button is by its original, most humble and true nature, created to fulfil a role, be it functional or decorative. It can be touching and full of past resonance to see how things are cut down, mended, adjusted and brought into new service in our lives, made to fight another day.

The same lesson of adaptability in one's own life, unless one is extraordinarily fortunate, may fairly be applied to buttons. A parallel might further be drawn with old buildings. Edward Hollis discusses the possibilities that open up when a building that has become defunct is adapted to some new purpose and gains new life in the process. In like manner a single button from an eighteenth-century set, rather than being shut away safely from possible injury, may be worn and enjoyed, as a piece of jewellery, say.

The button is measured in *lignes*, sometimes referred to as 'lines' or 'L', 40 lines equalling one inch. Buttonholes can be edged with stitching or bound with fabric. With modern stretch fabrics that do not tend to fray, or when a frayed effect is desired, a buttonhole can be a stitch-less slash, or machined round millimetres from the edges to keep the edges firm. Some seemingly malevolent buttonholes will never seem to retain a button properly, puckering and allowing the button to slip out, come what may. The buttonhole, designed to allow for movement, can become unreliable, holding the button yet allowing it to slip and slide about. Tristram Shandy, in the novel of that name, teases the reader by promising all manner of delights with

37. Sumptuous blue silk waistcoat, 1740–9, embroidered with silver thread, sequins and ornamental buttons on the pocket flap. Blue and silver were fashionable in the eighteenth century for gentlemen, Samuel Richardson's Mr B. wearing such for his marriage to Pamela.

a never-realized chapter on buttonholes, the movement of the button suggesting to him the passage of a human life:

> What is the life of man? Is it not to shift from side to side? – from sorrow to sorrow? – to button up one cause of vexation, – and unbutton another?
>
> (Laurence Sterne, *Tristram Shandy*, 1759, Vol. 1, ch. 117)

Sometimes a missing button may seem to suggest a certain integrity, as when Heidi Moore describes Goldman Sachs executives as not dressing as one might expect of Wall Street bankers, but with 'frayed cuffs, baggy suits and lost buttons' (Friedman, 2009). Their disarray reassures the public that they have better things to think about than mere appearance – or possibly that they have deservedly fallen upon hard times. Undone buttons can suggest unworldliness or even madness (see Chapter 1).

Buttons can keep upholstery in place, as with felt mattress buttons and their inner toggles, and add decorative definition. Sometimes the length and colour of the thread that attaches such buttons is made deliberately visible, mimicking quilting on oriental silk jackets, like scarlet whiskers on a dark matt silk pelt. Quilters will use all manner of button and button-like additions to add definition to their work. Upholstery buttons are used chiefly on chairs, including the all-over buttoned, low-backed Chesterfield couch (named after the same Earl of Chesterfield who offered advice to his son on gentlemanly attitudes to dress), or the high-backed winged armchair, on cushions and sometimes quilted pelmets, to add a quality of generous opulence yet maintaining an overall staunch solidity. Sitting in such chairs, the

38. Sofa, nineteenth-century rococo revival, of carved rosewood with deep-buttoned, mulberry silk upholstery.

impression the buttons make on the back of one's legs, and across one's back can become imprinted on the memory. Grayson Perry recalls his stepfather in the 1970s through such an image: 'there was a vinyl sofa in cracked cream vinyl studded with five flat buttons' (Jones and Perry, 2006, cited at www.vam.ac.uk). Velvet buttoned upholstery may suggest Victorian values, lavish but dusty, and thoroughly buttoned-up. In contrast there are the deeply glamorous buttoned leather seats on 'Black Bess', a five-litre Bugatti sports car commissioned by the French aviator and fighter pilot Roland Garros before the First World War – but which he never drove, as he was shot down in 1918.

The 'bellybutton' is a term used for the navel, the scar in the centre of the abdomen where the umbilical cord was once attached in the womb, the lateral umbilical ligament, the remains of what was once an essential artery. The scan of a foetus in uterus has very much the appearance of a button attached by its umbilical shank to the mother garment. Lately there has been a fashion for piercing bellybuttons with a jewellery button bar. Navels commonly form a slight depression, and are sometimes known as 'innies', but more unusually the umbilical cord has been awkwardly clamped and healed less than neatly and the resulting slight protuberance, or 'outie', can cause embarrassment or even shame.

There are claims that some people have no bellybutton at all, or so little that they have been termed 'smoothies'. Presumably Adam and Eve would not have had one at all. Many premature babies turn out to have relative 'smoothies', as do babies born by caesarean section. Frontally conjoined twins are also deficient in deep or pronounced navels. An absence may be the result of other early gastric operations. A relatively smooth indentation has led to suspicion of people being alien, or at any rate is often felt to give an 'unnatural' appearance. In fact it might be argued that the un-knotty bellybutton is rather more natural, in that it may be the result of the umbilical chord being left to shrivel and fall away, as with many animals. Such natural childbirth practice is termed a 'lotus' birth, from Hindu mythology, or umbilical non-severance birth. Adults sometimes lose their bellybuttons after abdominal surgery.

Such is the anxiety absent bellybuttons can induce that even supermodels lacking sufficient scarring are said to have to have them airbrushed onto their photographs. Various celebrities are suspected of like absences, and paparazzi vie to catch an image of a mutant stomach, like a medieval search for the mark of the devil. However, plastic surgery is not usually thought advisable. Rajiv Grover, consultant plastic surgeon and secretary of the British Association of Aesthetic Plastic Surgeons, told the BBC in 2009 that such fabricated scarring can pull and tighten over time, though it can work well after a hernia operation or tummy tuck, when surplus skin and fat can help form a successful substitute.

In Japanese mythology the soul is said to escape through the bellybutton, so that care should be taken when under frontal attack. In Hindu cosmology a lotus with a thousand petals sprouts from the bellybutton of Vishnu, in the very centre of which sits Brahma, the creator. In this context the bellybutton becomes the centre of the universe, a microcosm of everything, the *axis mundi*, and symbolizes both the feminine through the umbilical chord and the masculine through the male role in procreation.

Hesokuri, or 'bellybutton money', is a term for the stash of money that a Japanese housewife, and sometimes husband, may hoard in secret in case of future need. A perennial joke revolves around women who forget where they have hidden such emergency funds.

American political buttons from the 1820s to 1840s include small waistcoat buttons showing the crossed flags of the Union. Printed portraits of the Civil War generals were produced under mica, some also bearing the spread eagle motif. The first political campaign for the presidency to incorporate buttons in any quantity was the Harrison – Van Burren contest in 1840, in which Harrison was represented by the image of a log cabin. It is said that there were three versions, to please all: one with a central barrel of cider, to please all hard drinkers; another with the barrel to one side of the cabin, to appeal to moderate drinkers; the last had no barrel at all. Another notable image is that of a green frog, symbolizing the 1862 Federal Government issue of large amounts of non-interest bearing treasury notes, known as greenbacks, instead of legal tender. Some say the frog was also intended to denote the erratic gambling that greenbacks encouraged.

In the United States the word 'button' may more readily denote a political campaign pin or brooch, and follow on from stick pins and lapel studs as emblems of allegiance. There are such button-badges representing every point of view. Quickly and cheaply produced, they invite the whacky and the marginal viewpoint. Button-badges were made possible by the invention of a simple mechanical means of production, involving trapping a thin paper disc, protected by a disc of plastic, between a metal base and collar which clamped down to hold all in place. The process developed by the New Jersey firm of Whitehead and Hoag in the 1890s works on the same principle as buttons on dungarees or the fastenings for stocking and sock suspenders, save that the button-badge is permanently fixed in place. Philip Attwood (2004) makes the point that North American politics tended to be more central- ized than British politics, thus making the widespread dis- semination of electoral images more financially viable, and ultimately more effective in their influence. It is also per- haps true that politics, in the UK at least, remains some- thing that people feel more distanced from and thus less willing to openly demonstrate their allegiances than their American counterparts.

Some of the button-badges most sought after by collec- tors tend to be the runs that were never distributed, such as those buttons proper made for the coronation that never was of Edward VIII in Britain, and for campaigns that were of necessity secret, as with those button-badges worn by the Ku Klux Klan or members of the ANC before the fall of apartheid. Short runs might be affordable and could be eas- ily and quickly produced. To wear a button-badge demon- strating one's disapproval of the Vietnam conflict in the early 1960s invited being accused of disloyalty and might risk one's personal safety, whereas when the war became more gener- ally unpopular, they became a much easier badge of honour.

The political button-badge can thus become a bludg- eoning force for the majority view, albeit within distinct opinion groups. In totalitarian countries it can help shore up support as with Mao button-badges in China and Russian Stalin and Lenin button-badges; in contrast, in liberal democracies the wearing of a large collection often of conflicting viewpoints can betray the nerd (Lurie, 1981, p. 23), or in the case of say the Hell's Angel anarchist, a chance to cock a snook at politics in general.

Madeleine Albright reports wearing hot-air balloon pins to subtly demonstrate her view of foreign policy in general: 'You need the helium to get it up, and you need the ballast to give it direction' (*The New Yorker*, 5 October 2009), recalling the time when fashionable men about town were wearing sets of Parisian silver Montgolfier brothers' buttons, to celebrate their first successful voyage in 1783, and to show their affinity with modernity. Albright's pins are too elaborate to be deemed button-badges, but her love of matching mood or event with suitable pin exhibits similar motives. Button-badges, unlike buttons, tend to be forthright in their message, in some ways representing the cultural shift in attitudes between the old world and the new, where American principles of speaking one's mind and 'cutting the crap' are held in esteem, as against European evasion.

The button-badge is also widely worn as demonstrating an affiliation to a hobby or club membership, a sexual affiliation or ecological value. Any and every image can be acquired: of a favourite domestic animal, pop star, or to make a case for one's sense of humour. In American politics, humour and kitsch are sometimes finely balanced, as for example when a delegate wears a cap covered in button-badges decorated with lavatories, to express his feeling about what has happened to the economy. The message is clear but intended to be witty. Such button-badges can be used as a mean private joke by the originators, such as those I saw being sold to Japanese students whose grasp of English idiom was limited: 'A BUTTON SHORT', providing an insult to both stature and intellect.

Historically, the political button in America initially became a tool that candidates might use to gain favour after suffrage was extended in the 1820s, when all white men were given the vote. The very first campaign button-badge commemorated George Washington's inauguration in

1789. Washington did not campaign, as he was not entirely willing to seek the premiership, but clothing buttons were worn at the inauguration with his name printed on them, and these became the design for the newly available badges. The Gilman Collection houses a rare daguerreotype button showing a photograph of two children's hands, one over the other, one black, one white, and assumed to be resting on a copy of the Bible. It has a gilt frame and a simple loop at the back to attach with a pin – and it is as eloquent as any fine-tuned political speech.

In all, the Smithsonian Museum houses 30,000 political buttons. Jennifer Kabat sites African-American women in 1868 in the southern states walking miles to get Republican buttons, since, although they had no vote, they wished to show their support for Republican President Lincoln, who had abolished slavery three years previously. On his first button for the 1904 election, Roosevelt was shown eating with Booker T. Washington; the button was entitled 'equality', and worn first by African-American men on their jacket lapels. Andrew Jackson is credited with initiating the donkey symbol of the Democratic Party, which his rivals were then able to lampoon on button-badges declaring 'Jackass'. By their nature such political messages tend to be forthright, but Kabat also gives examples of more subtle images, such as the small peanut button, which succinctly supported the cause of peanut farmer Jimmy Carter. It is said that Richard Nixon campaigned with separate buttons for each and every ethnic group, presumably carefully choreographed depending on his target audience. Of the many logos for Barack Obama, Harry Rubenstein of the Smithsonian backs the simplicity of the small simple 'O' button as standing the best chance of gaining iconic status.

Eventually I come to that most pervasive example of the button any Internet search organ will turn up: the virtual button. Buttons have been shown to have diverse symbolic meanings, but here is a symbol, an icon on a screen, that looks like a button and takes on many of the characteristics associated with buttons, and is even promoted to appeal to some of the affections into which the button taps. They are used as virtual navigation switches, and the Internet offers ways of importing and creating new symbols from scratch. It may add interactivity to a film, respond to mouse clicks and help one to read and restructure a Web page.

Much of the terminology surrounding computers tends towards the board game or childish pursuit, perhaps derived from the enthusiasm of the original developers, but partly I suspect to humanize what at first seems alien. To name just a few of the many button idioms surrounding such technology, a 'button masher' is one who presses the controls of a video game at random, a 'button monkey' someone who has a mindless job pushing buttons for his boss, a 'button salad' refers to a Web page with all too many different styles of virtual button on screen and to be 'button happy' is to hit the keys of your mobile telephone with wild abandon while messaging.

Many modern computer and Internet associated artefacts, like mobile phones and iPods, have gradually become comforting, much-handled objects, and their concomitant vocabulary and their button-like keys are similarly reassuring. We are connected to satellites and a vast spectrum of other social worlds through the media of these little screens with their buttons, virtual or otherwise. Even fine art we have seen created thereby. We may not be able to draw, speak Hindi, write music, make friends, make love, even torture and kill at will, yet suddenly with the click of a button all these things appear to be possible.

In the practical world computer technology continues to extend its range. One instance is a minute digital button that can be attached to the clothes of dementia patients, containing the patients' names and room numbers and so helping to prevent any potential distress if these are mislaid. Health staff may be issued with buttons which use mobile phone technology to help locate patients, and so increase the patients' safety. Some trains, buses and city centres have been given alarm systems using similar technology, though such schemes have not proved entirely successful. Confused tourists press 'panic' buttons hoping for travel advice; in Belfast five emergency contact points were set up but were largely used by pranksters. In schools 'bully' buttons have been introduced, to discreetly record threatening incidents. The huge range of technological buttons may add to our sense of the button in general being a helpful or sometimes intrusive notion. People talk of 'help' buttons, and websites which do not have them, particularly if they are used by children or other vulnerable sectors of society, are frowned upon. The Online Protection Centre CEOP advises all such sites to adopt their Report Button. This insistence on immediate touch-button help can tend to increase one's level of anxiety and tends towards infantilizing the agent. Sites such as Facebook and all the numerous possibilities of Twitter lead to claims of cyber-bullying, being unduly influenced or being led astray – and yet again only a virtual button can help us.

Since this has been a book about buttons something should perhaps be said about the business of how to attach a button and even how to make a button or two. Buttons have a habit of getting lost, so it is as well to learn the basic skill. It can be only too obvious which button has been replaced, so try to match the thread colour and manner of stitching. If this is not possible then you should replace all the buttons.

When attaching a four-holed button, there are several patterns you can make, crosswise, in two parallel lines, a square of connecting lines or three into one forming an arrow or flower shape. Choose the gauge of your thread with care, matching the relative strength of the fabric. Avoid using a knot, since it can become unravelled, particularly if coming under any strain: begin with a few tiny stitches back and forth instead. The most important aspect according to best tailoring practice is, bearing in mind the thickness of your cloth, that you leave a sufficient and even shank between cloth and button. If this proves difficult to achieve you may place a match or some such, between the two while sewing. In most cases you should wind the thread several times round the shank, and perhaps add a blanket stitch or two before finishing off on the underside, by running a few stitches back and forth as before.

Two buttons to make:

1. Cloth button: take a scrap of coarse cotton or linen about 2 inches square. Draw a circle of 1.25 inches in diameter inside and sew a running thread round its circumference; pull up gently, tucking the edges inside to create the stuffing. Make several stitches in a cross pattern on the back to secure and create a shank.

2. Thread or yarn button: find a curtain ring, some scraps of wool and lengths of embroidery thread. With a darning needle wind a length of wool all round the ring, securing by weaving back under the bound wool; with a length of thread, stitch back and forward across the circle, working round gradually back and forth, as with the motion of a Spirograph toy, until

the ring is filled in. This can be done neatly, but even roughly achieved the effect can be attractive. Finish off by forming a shank on one side as with (1).

This book on the button has turned into something of a maze, where to follow one path for too long means one neglects another – yet its purpose has been not to escape the button, but rather to bring the threads together into something whole, very much as with the simplified version of the Dorset button above. I am left with the impression that most of civilized life turns in some small way upon the button. And so I shall finish off with a quote from Beryl Bainbridge that buttons up well these various strands: Dr Johnson tells a tale of one Saltmarsh, who drags a drowned man from the Serpentine in Hyde Park, London, with the help of his dog. The dog worries away at the corpse's buttons and eventually some cloth tears away with 'one silver button catching the sunlight'. The animal hurriedly buries it and then sits across it 'like a hen on an egg':

At the close of the story, Dr Johnson observed, 'Without buttons we are all undone'.

(Beryl Bainbridge, *According to Queeney*, 2001)

39. Michelle Holmes, dark grey machine embroidery on linen buttons, 2008.

NOTES

CHAPTER 1

1   Arthur Schopenhauer, *The World as Will and Representation*, Vol. 1, trans. E. F. J. Payne (New York: Dover Publications, 1966), section 47.

2   Alison Lurie holds that the clothes we wear are a means of communication. We may not be able to articulate our responses and we may not wear a wide variety of styles ourselves, but this does not mean that, at some level, we do not share in a language of clothes. She suggests that items of clothing constitute the vocabulary of dress with its own grammar. In relation to the button she argues that 'A case can be made... for considering trimmings and accessories as adjectives or adverbs – modifiers in the sentence that is the total outfit...'.

CHAPTER 3

1   Parole in the linguistic sense, of something spoken or written as opposed to a system of shared understanding, or *langue* (see Ferdinand de Saussure).

2   Madeleine Ginsberg cites Adam Smith visiting the Birmingham works in *Lectures on Justice, Police, Revenue and Arms*, 1896: 'a person's whole attention is bestowed on the eightieth part of a button so far divided are these manufactures'.

CHAPTER 4

1 During the first screening of *Death in Venice*, at a moment of great tension, when Dirk Bogarde, playing von Aschenbach, is staring longingly at Tadzio, a beautiful young boy, and the cinema is silent with anticipation, Tom Wolfe writes in a preface to Epstein and Safro, 'out of the darkness came the unmistakable contralto stage-whisper of the wife of one of New York's best-known dress designers: "Look, Darling! Those buttons! To die!" '.

CHAPTER 7

1 The *sakoku* policy ran from 1635 to 1853, during which time the penalty was death for any foreigner daring to enter Japan; the same penalty applied until the Meiji Restoration in 1868 for any Japanese attempting to leave Japan.

The Reform Bills of 1832, 1867 and 1884, in their gradual attempt to extend the vote, expose just how small a percentage of society was able to partake in fashion and thus were able to make choices with regard to buttons.

The Factory Acts were extended between 1860 and 1878 to cover a wide variety of occupations including, after 1861, button making and associated dye works, steel manufacture and the potteries.

GLOSSARY

Ajouré	perforated or pierced-work button
Basket	woven effect, sometimes using hair
Casein	(a.k.a. Erinoid or Galalith) an early form of plastic, good at imitating natural materials and accepting dye
Cheese-plate	extremely large, in relation to a button
Cloisonné	design technique using flattened wire outlines laid on edge and then filled in with coloured enamels
Corozo	seed of a tropical American palm tree
Daguerrotype	one of earliest photographic processes where an image is produced on iodine-sensitized silver and developed in mercury vapour
Diamanté	decorated with glittering ornament, such as artificial jewels or sequins
Églomisé	or *verre églomisé*, an ancient technique revived by the French eighteenth-century picture-frame maker Glomy, which involved etching into a painted gold or silver layer on the back of glass, then painting over with black pigment
Ferrotype	or tintype, photographic print produced in camera, by exposing sheet of iron or tin coated with sensitized enamel
Foil	very thin layer of metal, or small gold and silver forms
Goofy	see *Realistic*
Guilloché	type of enamelwork, where enamel is poured into an engraved bed

Habitat	eighteenth-century technique where moss, grass and insects are held under glass to depict natural scenes
Horn	more often hoof, shipped to Britain from Europe to the Birmingham factories, often arriving as a stinking mass, rotten with maggots
Jasperware	Wedgwood stoneware decorated with raised classical decoration
Jennens	and Co, London, manufacturers of military and uniform buttons, 1800s–1924
Kachina	supernatural beings, Hopi American Indian ancestral spirits
Kagagami-buta	centre of round *netsuke*, ivory body with metal, often brass lid, sometimes inlaid with gold and silver
Lacy glass	glass buttons made in handmade iron moulds, sometimes back-painted, sometimes with added lustres
Lava	from Vesuvius, often carved in Italy into cameos bearing classical heads
Macaroni	eighteenth-century English dandy, affecting a continental manner
Manju	flattened round *netsuke*, usually made of wood, ivory or horn
Passementerie	fretwork in metallic thread over a wooden mould, often trimmed with jewels, beads, mirrors, sequins
Paste	hard shiny glass, imitating gems
Pietra dura	'hard stone', as in Florentine mosaic
Realistic	buttons made in realistic shapes, usually in plastics
Ryusa	flattened sphere-shaped *netsuke*, hollow with intricate design carved through to the centre
Satsuma	type of Japanese porcelain
Scarab	dried scarab beetle, regarded by the ancient Egyptians as divine, often made in ceramic replica
Shank	stem or ring at the back of a button, sometimes made of linen or sewn threads,

	sometimes of leather or metal. The latter come in many forms: for example, simple loop, birdcage, box shank
Sinkies	children's game played with buttons, similar to marbles, with different values being given to different types of button
Strass	German term for paste or lead-glass cut as gemstones
Tombac	metal alloys, usually copper, tin and zinc
Trompe l'oeil	a painting or effect that gives the illusion of reality

BIBLIOGRAPHY

BUTTONS

Andrews, John H. 'Hair-painted Buttons'. *Journal of the National Button Society of America*. www.ogosh-buttons.com/hair (*National Button Bulletin*, 1955).

Epstein, Diana. *The Button Book*. Philadelphia and London: Running Press, 1996.

Epstein, Diana and Safro, Millicent. *Buttons*. New York: Harry N. Abrams, 1991.

Farrow, Jan. 'Suffragette Buttons'. *Button Lines. Journal of the British Button Society* 138, March 2009.

Ginsburg, Madeleine. 'Buttons: Art and Industry'. *Apollo Magazine*, June 1977.

Herdman, Sue. 'Buttons and the Baroness'. *V&A Magazine*, November 2000.

Houart, Victor. *Buttons: A Collector's Guide*. London: Souvenir Press, 1985.

Hughes, Elizabeth and Lester, Marion. *The Big Book of Buttons*. Boyertown, PA: Boyertown Publishing Company, 1981.

Osborne, Peggy Anne. *About Buttons: A Collector's Guide*. Atglen, PA: Schiffer, 1994.

Perry, Jane. *A Collector's Guide to Peasant Silver Buttons*. Lulu Press, 2007.

Scarisbrick, Diana. 'Tales Told in Buttons'. *Country Life Magazine*, 11 February 1999.

GENERAL

Akita, Kimiko. 'The Sexual Commodification of Women in the Japanese Media', in Theresa Carilli, and Jane Campbell (eds), *Women and the Media: Diverse Perspectives*. Lanham, MD: University Press of America, 2005.

Anderson, Lee. 'The History of American Indian Jewelery'. www.americana.net.

Ariès, Philippe. *Centuries of Childhood: A Social History of Family Life*, trans. Robert Baldick. London: Pimlico, 1996.

Attwood, Philip. *Badges*. London: The British Museum Press, 2004.

Barthes, Roland. *The Fashion System*, trans. Matthew Ward and Richard Howard. Berkeley and Los Angeles: University of California Press, 1990.

Bell, Quentin. *On Human Finery*. London: Hogarth Press, 1976.

Bessborough, Earl of (ed.), *The Correspondence of Georgiana Duchess of Devonshire*. London: John Murray, 1955.

Binder, Pearl. *The Pearlies: A Social Record*. London: Jupiter Books, 1975.

Bradtke, Birgit. *The Colourful History of Broome and Its Pearling Industry*. Kimberley Travel Guide, 2006. Available at kimberleyaustralia.com.

Carlyle, Thomas. *Sartor Resartus: The Life and Opinions of Herr Teufelsdröckh*, ed. Kerry McSweeney and Peter Sabor. Oxford World Classics, Oxford: Oxford University Press, 2000 [1833–4].

Collins, Lauren. 'Big Pin', *New Yorker*, 5 October 2009.

Connerton, Paul. *How Societies Remember*. Cambridge: Cambridge University Press, 2009.

Copping, Nicola. 'My Life in Fashion: Grayson Perry', *The Times*, 12 December 2007.

Crill, Rosemary, Wearden, Jennifer and Wilson, Verity. *World Dress: Fashion in Detail*. London: V&A Publishing, 2009.

Crompton, Margaret. *George Eliot: The Woman*. Part I, New York: T. Yoseloff, 1960.

Cruickshank, Marjorie. *Children and Industry*. Manchester: Manchester University Press, 1981.

Dickman, A. J. 'The G I University in Shrivenham England', *The French Review*, American Association of Teachers of French, 1946.

Edwards, Peter. 'Cuteness, Kitsch and Paedomorphic Emotion.' *XIIIth International Conference of Aesthetics*, Lahti Finland, 1995.

Elsner, John and Cardinal, Roger. *The Cultures of Collecting*. London: Reaktion, 1994.

Flugel, John C. *Psychology of Clothes*. New York: AMS Press, 1966.

Friedman, Vanessa. 'Clothes maketh the Goldman', *Financial Times*, 25 October 2009.

Fugitani, Takashi, White, Geoffrey Miles and Yoneyama, Lisa. *Perilous Memories: The Asia-Pacific Wars*. Durham, NC: Duke University Press, 2001.

Grant, Linda. *The Thoughtful Dresser*. New York: Virago, 2009.

Guénon, René. *Introduction to the Study of the Hindu Doctrines*, trans. Sophia Perennis. Hillsdale, NY, 2001 [1945].

Haldane, Elizabeth-Anne. 'Surreal Semi-Synthetics', *V&A Magazine*, Spring 2007.

Hart, Avril and North, Susan. *Historical Fashion in Detail, 17th and 18th Centuries*. London: V&A Publications, 1998.

Hayman, Ronald. *The Death and Life of Sylvia Plath*. London: Heinemann, 1991.

Hayward, Catherine and Dunn, Bill. *Men About Town – The Changing Image of the Modern Male*. London: Hamlyn, 2001.

Hillstaff, Justin. 'Button Theft Brings Heartache to Storeowner', *Oakland Tribune*, 11 April 2007.

Hollander, Ann. *Seeing through Clothes*. New York: Viking, 1978.

Hollis, Edward. *The Secret Lives of Buildings*. London: Portobello Books, 2009.

Jones, Wendy and Perry, Grayson. *Grayson Perry: Portrait of the Artist as a Young Girl*. London: Chatto and Windus, 2006.

Kabat, Jennifer. 'All Buttoned Up', *Frieze Magazine*, 29 August 2008.

Kite, Marion and Hill, Audrey. 'The Conservation and Mounting of a Jinbaori', *V&A Conservation Journal*, April 1998.

Knight, Kevin. 'Clerical costume', in *New Advent, Catholic Encyclopedia*. New York: Robert Appleton, 2009.

Kukil, Karen V. (ed.) *The Unabridged Journals of Sylvia Plath*. New York: Anchor Books, 2000.

Latimer, Quinn. 'Elias Simé', *Frieze*, June–August 2009.

Lim, Louisa. 'Chinese "Button Town" Struggles with Success', *National Public Radio*, 22 August 2006.

Livesay, Beth. 'Faded Beauty: The Artwork of Priscilla Jones', *Somerset Studio Magazine*, July/August 2009.

Lurie, Alison. *The Language of Clothes*. London: Bloomsbury, 1981.

Mack, John. *The Art of Small Things*. London: The British Museum Press, 2007.

McCabe, Susan. *Elizabeth Bishop Her Poetics of Loss*. University Park: Pennsylvania State University Press, 1994.

Mikhaila, Ninya and Malcolm-Davies, Jane. *The Tudor Tailor*. London: BT Batsford, 2000.

Nowottony, Winifred. *The Language Poets Use*. London: The Athalone Press, 1965.

Papanek, Victor. *The Green Imperative: Natural Design for the Real World*. New York: Thames & Hudson, 1995.

Quick, Harriet. 'Craft Work (Charlotte Stockdale)', *British Vogue*, April 2007.

Rhodes, Zandra and Knight, Anne. *The Art of Zandra Rhodes*. Philadelphia, PA: Trans-Atlantic Publications, 1995.

Ryan, Michael. *Literary Theory*. Oxford: Blackwell, 2007.

Sayers, D. L. *The Image of God*. London: Methuen, 1941.

Schellman, Jörg and Klüser, Bernd. *Joseph Beuys: The Multiples*. New York: Harvard University Art Museums, Walker Art Centre, 1997.

Schopenhauer, Arthur. *The World as Will and Representation*, Vol. 1, trans. E. F. J. Payne. New York: Dover Publications, 1966.

Steele, Valerie. *The Corset: A Cultural History*. New Haven, CT: Yale University Press, 2001.

Stemp, Sinty. *Jean Muir: Beyond Fashion*. Woodbridge, Suffolk: Antique Collector's Club, 2006 [1988].

Stewart, Susan. *On Longing, Narratives of the Miniature, the Gigantic, the Souvenir, the Collection*. Durham, NC and London: Duke University Press, 1993.

Strong, Roy. *Gloriana: The Portraits of Queen Elizabeth I*. London: Thames and Hudson, 1987.

Strong, Roy and Trevelyan Oman, Julia. *Elizabeth R*. Indiana University: Stein and Day, 1971.

Thackeray, W. M. *The History of Pendennis: His Fortunes and Misfortunes, His Friends and His Greatest Enemy*. London: Macmillan, 1925 [1848–50].

Veblen, Thorstein. *Theory of the Leisure Class*. New York: Penguin Classics, 1994 [1899].

Vinken, Barbara. *Fashion Zeitgeist: Trends and Cycles in the Fashion System*. Oxford: Berg, 2005.

Zak, Dan. 'Amalia Amaki: Ladies Sing the Blues', *Washington Post*, 11 June 2005.

Ziemke, Earl F. 'The US Army in the Occupation of Germany, 1944–1946'. Washington, DC: GPO, Center of Military History, United States Army, 1990. Available at www.history.army.mil/books/wwii/occ-gy/ch18.

Zipser, Helga H. 'Netsuke, Japan's Miniature Treasures', *Antiques and Art around Florida*, Winter/Spring 1996.

WEBSITES

www.anncarrington.co.uk (Ann Carrington)
www.archangelstudio.co.uk (Michelle Holmes)
www.artangel.org.uk (Artangel for Charles Ledray)
www.britishbuttonsociety.org (British Button Society)
www.elisabethlecourt.com (Elisabeth Lecourt)
www.galeriebesson.co.uk (Galerie Besson)
www.heatherwick.com (Thomas Heatherwick)
www.janeburchcochran.com (Jane Burch Cochran)
www.judithbrownjewellery.co.uk (Judith Brown)
www.lucyqdesigns.co.uk (Lucy Quartermaine)
www.modernartistsgallery.com (Kate Kessling)
www.nationalbuttonsociety.org (National Button Society, America)
www.priscillajones.co.uk (Priscilla Jones)
www.raycaesar.com (Ray Caesar)
www.ranhwang.com (Ran Hwang)
www.thebuttonqueen.co.uk (Martyn Frith)
www.vandenbosch.co.uk (Van Den Bosch)
www.victoria-miro.com (Grayson Perry)
www.zandrarhodes.com (Zandra Rhodes)

INDEX